PLAYMATES OF THE TOWPATH

Charles Ludwig

PLAYMATES OF THE

TOWPATH

Happy Memories of the Canal Swimmers' Society

© 1929 by Charles Ludwig.
© 2019 by Commonwealth Book Company.
All Rights Reserved.
Printed in the United States of America.

**Dedicated
to All the
Playmates**

How This Book Came To Be

When the old canal was replaced by the beautiful new Central Parkway, a committee from the Parkway requested Moses Strauss, managing editor of The Times-Star, to have some special articles prepared calling attention to the dedication of the boulevard, October 1, 2 and 3, 1928.

This pleasant task was assigned to the writer. Having been an enthusiastic canal swimmer as a boy, it occurred to him that the launching of a Canal Swimmers' Society, founded on happy memories of youthful days, and the publication of canal yarns would accomplish the desired purpose. All who ever swam, fished, boated, skated or played along the canal were eligible to join the society, and girls who had as much as thrown sticks or stones into the canal could also become members.

The society and the canal yarns aroused widespread public interest and revived delightful memories for thousands of Cincinnatians. Men and women joined the society in great numbers and sent a flood of letters relating their happy canal reminiscences. Letters came from all parts of Cincinnati and all sections of the United States, from New York, Los Angeles, Pennsylvania, Iowa, Florida, Michigan, Kentucky, from Cuba, Panama, Nicaragua—from all places where there are former Cincinnatians who had known the canal.

It was amazing with what affection they looked back upon their old swimming hole! High and low, rich and poor became members of the Canal Swimmers' Society—Speaker Nicholas Longworth of the House of Representatives, Governor Myers Y. Cooper, Mayor Murray Seasongood, Congressman William E. Hess joined, together with distinguished business leaders, manufacturers, clerks, union members, mechanics, laborers—and all sent in jolly canal reminiscences.

The large and popular role the towpath played in Cincinnati's juvenile life is indicated by the fact that at The Times-Star alone interesting canal reminiscences were related by Mr. Charles P. Taft and Mr. Hulbert Taft, Mr. C. H. Rembold, general manager; Mr. George Fries, assistant general manager; Mr. Strauss, the managing editor; Mr. Edward Steinborn, city editor, and men from every department of the paper.

With the assistance of friends at the Public Library and all over the city and country the writer gathered together a large amount of canal data—photographs, history, stories—a collection such as would probably never again be assembled. The Times-Star desired to preserve this unique phase of Cincinnati life and offers it as an interesting contribution to the city's history, as was the case with Frank Y. Grayson's "Pioneers of Night Life on Vine Street," and in this spirit Mr. Fries proceeded with the publicaton of the book.

To those who loaned photographs or contributed stories or drawings, to the men who generously co-operated in preparing type and pictures and printing the book and to all who lent their assistance, the Canal Scribe wishes to express his sincere thanks.—The Author.

PLAYMATES OF THE TOWPATH

Oft to the canal we trooped as boys,
Shouting and laughing—what sweet noise!
"Follow the leader!"—blithe and gay—
The start of a perfect Towpath Day.

"Who'll jump in first?" Now there's a dash!
Clothes pulled off fast! Kerplunk! A splash!
Out of the water there pops a face,
Radiant in smiles— He Won the Race!

A canal boat comes! Hurrah! What fun!
To dive clear under, then to run
Atop the bridge, and oh! how grand!
To leap into the load of sand!

Some lads tie knots—a little prank—
In all the clothing on the bank!
"Now 'chaw' green apples!" shouts the bunch—
For hungry boys a wretched lunch.

"Cheese it, the cops!" the dreadful cry!
Lads seize their togs—away they fly!
While there appear, in fearsome awe,
The Faithful Guardians of the Law.
. . . . . .
Oh, white and glistening, icy path,
Cold blizzards freeze you in their wrath,
But warm young hearts and sprightly feet
Skate blithely toward a far retreat.

Through sylvan dales, how swift they glide!
A lovely moon! A blissful ride!
A lover sighs: "How wondrous nice!"
Then, cruel luck—breaks through the ice.
. . . . . .
Farewell, Towpath, Friend to us all!
In summer, winter, spring and fall,
Our Happy Playground all year through
And good-by Playmates! Luck to you!
. . . . . .
THE CANAL IS GONE! YET, HOW ALIVE!
HAIL! NEW AND MATCHLESS TOWPATH DRIVE!

Charles Ludwig.

BUSY SCENE ALONG CANAL IN THE SEVENTIES; PLUM STREET BEND, LOOKING SOUTH

*How dear to my heart are the scenes of my childhood,
When fond recollection presents them to view!*

HELLO! And welcome, Playmates of the Towpath!

Gather up close on the canal bank once more, members and friends of the Canal Swimmers' Society; there's a mighty crowd!

For this is to be our last happy meeting on the shores of our dear old Swimming hole.

A meeting consisting of Sweet Memories of the days of youth, Joyous Reminiscences, Delightful Retrospections—precious souvenirs and keepsakes enshrined in your Halls of Recollection.

Our Swimming Hole, yes, an entire city's swimming hole! And Playground, too, for over a hundred thousand of Cincinnati's boys and girls.

Ten miles of placid stretch of water through crowded tenements and pretty suburban districts of the city—for diving, swimming, fishing, boating, skating!

Twenty miles of canal banks for playing all the games of youth—mimic battles, bonfires, shinny, baseball, "two feet away," "follow the leader!"

Scores of bridges, built, it seems, just so that boys would have a high place to jump from!

Ah, the thrill of diving from a bridge into the water, or leaping off, daringly, to a passing canal boat for a free ride! Or of clinging, submerged, to the boat's rudder!

And the panic and flight when the dreaded cry: "Cheese it! The cop!" rent the air. We don't want this final session broken up, so we'll send a few outposts for lookout duty right now.

Recall, with us, the jolly Sunday picnics and excursions on old canal boats—with music and wonderful refreshments!

Outings to Second Basin, Mummert's Basin, Blair's Basin, in the lovely rural regions of the canal!

Holidays at Ross Lake, fishing, swimming and camping out over night!

The lad who tried to swim with air-bags tied to his feet—and was nearly drowned—feet up in the air, head down!

The beautiful waterfalls at Cumminsville!

Paddling grandly in your homemade canoe, till some boy dropped a stone off a bridge and sank your canvas ship!

Swimming, and rowing and skating contests!

Diving, and getting stuck, head first, in the mud!

The evening skiff riders, with their sweethearts and their serenades! Yes, thousands of girls, too, enjoyed playdays along the canal.

Steam launches laden with jolly excursionists—and heavy barrels!

The many exciting rescues—the tots that fell in; and the skating boys and girls that broke through the ice!

The strange roar of the waters, downtown, where they turned mill-wheels!

The lad whose heavy homemade experimental life preserver carried him to the bottom!

The quaint canal boats, with their neat curtains at the cabin windows, their slow and patient mules, their boatmen!

The sand-boats, the ice-boats, the daily whiskey packet boat and the electric mule.

The historic old City Hospital, exposition building, Music Hall, Brighton House, the 1,250-foot-long exposition building over the canal for the 1888 "Centennial."

The barricaded canal bridge in the '84 Courthouse riot—the alarming midnight fires in great buildings along the canal.

So today the old-timers and many not so old see a vision of the faithful mule, at the end of a long rope, tugging a quaint, romantic old canal boat—but he is also tugging at their heart-strings.

"Oh, those were the good old days"—they all write—the days when they could play all day, and run and jump and swim. . . .

The days of their boyhood triumphs and tragedies!

Once more the timid girls look down at the boats from the bridge and get an imaginary ride, though it does seem to them as though they, too, were moving!

Once more the canal is a seething caldron of exuberant boys, splashing, shouting! See that diving boy come up with a tin can wedged onto his nose!

Once again the drunken carriage driver drives his happy party of Over-the-Rhine celebrators into the canal!

Once again the merry songs of the gondoliers are heard—the Fall Festival Fire Fighters are at it again!

There is the three-legged dog that can't swim. A mischievous boy throws him in. The boy who owns the dog leaps into the canal and saves the life of his pet.

Once again the canal is frozen over—the towpath is snow-white. Thousands of skaters, girls, too! And bonfires here and there along the shore.

A big dog is drowning in a hole out of which he can not climb—a brave skater takes off shoes and skates, risks his life, leaps in and saves the dog.

A child is drowning in the middle of the wintry canal. A schoolboy rushes through the crowd, swims to the middle of the canal, where the child disappeared, dives to the bottom, brings it up, saves its life—and receives a medal for heroism.

Summer and the canal boat clubs are out once again—skiffs, canoes, homemade steam launches—Sunday outings with the inevitable keg of lager.

Enjoy, with us, these and a thousand other memories of the days gone forever. For our swimming hole is dried up and vanished. In its place, a subway and a magnificent new boulevard.

TRAVELING BY CANAL PASSENGER BOAT EIGHTY YEARS AGO—E. L. HENRY'S FAMOUS PAINTING

Canal, 244 Miles Long, Costing $6,000,000, Was Mighty State Project Started in 1825

Building the Miami and Erie Canal, 244 miles, Cincinnati to Toledo, at a cost of $6,000,000, was a great Ohio enterprise of a century ago.

The famous pioneer Cincinnatian, Dr. Daniel Drake, urged the building of the canal as early as 1815. Micajah T. Williams of Cincinnati, canal enthusiast, presented his engineering report in 1822 and the Ohio Legislature authorized the construction of both the Miami and Erie and Ohio Canal in 1825. Williams and Alfred Kelley were appointed commissioners to survey the route of the canal. "Not only did Williams inspect every part of the line of the projected canal, but it was due to his personal efforts that the funds were raised by pledging the faith and credit of the State of Ohio," says the historian, C. T. Greve.

Ground was broken for the canal at Middletown in July, 1825. Gov. Dewitt Clinton of New York, father of canals, came as guest of honor, and the Cincinnati military organizations, the Hussars and Guards, acted as his escort. Gov. Clinton and Gov. Morrow of Ohio together threw the first spadefuls of earth and a delegation of prominent Cincinnatians attended the ceremonies.

The canal started at the Mad River near Dayton, descended the Big Miami Valley and then the Millcreek Valley to Cincinnati.

In 1827 the first canal boats traveled from the outskirts of Cincinnati to Middletown. By 1829 the canal was completed to Main street, Cincinnati. In 1830 excavations were started to connect the canal with the Ohio River. By 1831 the canal was extended from Main street across Deercreek, over which it passed by a large culvert. "There it was proposed that the canal should stop for a time, and the water power was leased along the borders of the line," says Greve. It had been estimated that a 3,000-cubic foot flow of water per minute in the canal would provide power to turn sixty millstones in its fall of fifty feet to high water in the river.

Greve adds:

"In 1834 the canal was sixty-seven miles long. It contained thirty-two locks from the bottom of the canal at Main street to low-water mark on the Ohio. The fall was 106.27 feet, which, with the 3.75 feet depth of water in the lower lock, made the entire lockage at Cincinnati 110 feet. To overcome this there were then building ten locks of eleven feet lift.

"The completion of the canal and its opening for business was an event of much greater importance than would be supposed from present conditions. Before that time the mud roads and river were the only sources of supply. . . . The canal assured a reliable and easy means of communication throughout the year. As a result Cincinnati took on a new life, business improved, real estate advanced in value and population increased rapdily."

The canal was completed through to Toledo in 1840 with an expenditure of $5,920,000.

Peak of traffic was reached on the canal in 1851, when the tolls collected reached their highest figure—$352,000. The importance of the canal at that time is indicated by the fact that the file of the old Cincinnati Times around 1850 gives daily reports of the receipts and shipments of merchandise on the canal. With the advent of the railroads the canals lost their prestige. Over half a century ago the Eggleston avenue section of the canal was run into a huge sewer under the street.

ROUNDING MOHAWK BEND; FAIRVIEW INCLINE IN DISTANCE—LOANED BY FRANK WILMES

Let's Take First Trip of 1827 Over Again! Canal Boat Had Bar! Press Praised Liquors!

Come on, boys, let's take the first canal boat ride of 1827 over again, on the wings of imagination!

The files of two old Cincinnati newspapers at the Public Library—the Gazette and the Crisis and Emporium—tell the interesting story of this important pre-Volstead economic event of Cincinnati's early history.

The Crisis and Emporium joyously informs its readers that the first two canal boats at Cincinnati, the Washington and Clinton, "are fine, commodious boats, with handsome cabins, neatly furnished and a bar well supplied with comforts." It praises the wonderful dinner that Mr. Hughes gave at Middletown to the party of Cincinnatians making the first boat ride, saying on December 3, 1827: "His liquors were no less the subject of admiration, as they were equal to any that could be set out in Cincinnati." By November, 1827, the canal was finished from a point four miles from

FIRST CANAL PICTURE HERE, IN EMPORIUM, NOVEMBER 26, 1827.

Cincinnati to Middletown. On November 1, 1827, appeared the first canal advertisement in the Crisis and Emporium. It read:

"Merchants and Farmers' Line on the Miami Canal.—The freight and passenger boats Washington, Isaac Poineer, Martin and Clinton, B. W. Ball, master, will leave Howell's Basin, four miles north of Cincinnati, hill road, at half past nine Friday morning. The party will spend the night at Hamilton, next morning proceed to Middletown, dine, and return to the basin, where carriages will be provided to accommodate the company. These boats are finished and furnished in an ample style calculated to afford satisfactory accommodations to passengers."

But an accident at the Millcreek aqueduct—the first canal accident here—caused the dedication trip to be postponed. The Emporium of November 5, 1827, thus tells about it:

"Miami Canal Accident.—An accident happened to the aqueduct across Millcreek. The upper wing of the wall, on the south side of the creek, gave way.

PURITAN BOAT CLUB, WITH FIRST STEAM LAUNCH ON CANAL, IN 1884—LOANED BY ARTHUR A. TAYLOR

"Prompt and immediate measures were adopted by the canal commissioner, M. T. Williams, to prevent an increased injury by the breach, and for its repair in two or three weeks. Two fine boats were advertised to leave yesterday morning for Middletown. A satisfactory trial of the boats was made over the aqueduct, under the bridges and through the locks the evening preceding the breach. A large number of men are employed repairing the breach."

On November 19 the Emporium reported that the work of repair at White's Mill was progressing rapidly and that the boats were again ready for a "pleasant excursion," and that "much credit is due the canal company for preparing such comfortable boats and easy means of traveling."

The break was repaired and the first boat ride to Middletown proved a complete success. The Emporium of December 3, 1827, under the heading, "The First Trip of the Canal Boats," described it thus:

"On Wednesday last the canal boats Washington and Clinton left Howell's Basin, four miles from the city, at 1 o'clock for Hamilton and Middletown. They had been previously fitted up in handsome style for a trip of pleasure and furnished equal to the steamboats on the Ohio River. Public curiosity was much excited as to the result of the 'successful experiment.' We are gratified to learn that the boats got under way at 1 o'clock and made good progress up the canal, with a band of music consisting of ten musicians and about sixty passengers. The progress was about four miles per hour, where there was a full head of water. The variety and amusements cheering to the passengers, and convivial humor served to enlighten the company whilst the boats moved steadily on. At 8 o'clock the boats arrived at Hamilton, where an excellent supper was prepared by Mr. Blair, and the company enjoyed themselves during the remainder of the evening. Thursday morning the Washington and Clinton proceeded on for Middletown with some increase of numbers. They arrived at 1 o'clock and shortly after the whole company sat down to a dinner prepared by Mr. Hughes in his commodious brick house. The passengers say for variety, taste and display, in fish, flesh, and fowl, there has not been a dinner got up in finer style in the State; the tasty arrangement reflects the greatest credit on Mr. Hughes; his liquors were no less the subject of admiration, as they were equal to any that could be set out in Cincinnati. His house will be a desirable resort for the convalescent, and others who may be going to or coming from Yellow Springs. The musical band, who kindly volunteered their services played a variety of airs going up and coming down, which contributed not a little to enliven the party.

"Among the passengers were the canal commissioner and engineer and a number of members of the Ohio Legislature on their way to Columbus, and several of our old citizens, who expressed their appreciation in the strongest terms, as to the satisfaction they felt in the success of boats going on this part of the canal. The members of the Legislature took their leave in high spirits, and proceeded on to Columbus. The boats received the lively cheers of the assemblage, as they took their departure for Hamilton and Cincinnati; they reached the basin on the afternoon of Friday, the company highly delighted with the attentions of the owners and officers of the boats, nothing having occurred to mar the pleasure of the excursion."

The Gazette of December 3 says a third boat, the Samuel Forrer, joined the expedition up the canal and that the average time in passing the locks was seven minutes.

Of the first public excursion on the canal the Gazette says, December 8:

"Canal Boat Washington, Capt. Poineer, will leave Howell's Basin a 11 a. m. on Monday on an Excursion of Pleasure and pass through the Reading locks and return the same day. Carriages can be obtained at the Washington Hall to carry passengers to the basin. The Washington will leave for Middletown at 10 a. m. Tuesday. Passage three cents per mile. Apply to the captain on board, or to W. D. Jones."

On December 12 the boat Clinton arrived at Howell's Basin from Middletown on probably her first business trip, with freight and passengers—the freight consisting of flour, whisky, pork and pork barrels to A. J. Gano.

On December 17 the papers announced that a third canal boat was ready to be launched and that contracts had been let for "a splendid passenger boat to be used exclusively for passengers."

READY FOR DIVE OFF BRIDGE! WADE STREET SWIMMING HOLE ON CANAL—WILMES PHOTO.

In Home-Made Life-Belt Hero Dove Alone, High Off the Bridge—But Sank Like Stone!

What's the funniest canal story?

When Edward J. Murphy, 758 Clark street, dove into the canal, years ago, hit bottom and came up with a tin can attached tightly to his nose, that was funny! He dived into the can.

But when Judd Brown, 9 Wesley avenue, resplendent in a home-made life preserver, dived off the Twelfth street bridge and failed to come up at all, that seems funnier—today!

But it was a mighty serious thing when it happened—Judd was nearly drowned.

The beer-soaked cork life preserver, made as an experiment by the Wesley avenue gang of boys, pulled Judd down to the bottom like a belt of lead, and held him there.

It was a real case of "spurlos versenkt!"

All that the frightened boys on the bank saw was bubbles coming up where Judd went down.

But a fireman leaped in and saved Judd's life.

Walter G. Reemelin, Dixie Terminal Building, helped make the nearly fatal life preserver, and tells the story.

AH! "DIAMOND DICK"

"Our gang had been reading 'Diamond Dick' and 'Nick Carter'," he writes. "We saw a picture of a life preserver in those books. It had cork belt and cork suspenders around the shoulders.

"We made a life preserver out of beer-soaked cork, heavy as iron, that we got from Gerke's Brewery. We were only 8 or 9, and thought that, as long as we had cork, we had a good life preserver. We did not know that weight had anything to do with it.

"We debated as to who should test our masterly creation. We could all swim. Just then Brownie came along. His parents gave him a nickel a day for spending money—a fortune.

"We said that for a nickel we would let him make the great test and win the glory of being a hero.

" 'But I can't swim!' he said.

"We showed him the picture of a life preserver in the magazine and said:

" 'So much the better. You jump from the bridge. It will scare all the people. We will save your life—you will be a hero.'

"We got his nickel and we put the life preserver on him. He stood on the bridge—and someone gave him a push.

"Down he went into the water. He disappeared below the surface and failed to come up! The heavy life preserver was holding him down and taking his life—he was stuck below in the mud!

SAW ONLY BUBBLES!

"All we saw was bubbles coming up where he went down. We kids went in to try to save him—but hadn't it been for the timely arrival of a

CANAL WINTER SCENE AT MOHAWK—FOOTE'S BEAUTIFUL PAINTING, 1882—IN CINCINNATI CLUB

city fireman, who waded in and and pulled Brownie out, he would be up with the angels now.

"When they pulled him out he had mud over his shoetops. He had swallowed half the canal.

"While bringing him out the fireman said: 'What's the big idea with that contraption around you?' Between gulps and heaves of canal water he told him it was '—a life preserver!'—but he guessed he 'didn't have it on right!' The corks were like pig iron!"

Now Reemelin writes:

"Your Canal Swimmers' Society is a knockout. Can I get in?"

Not only is he admitted as a charter member, but is appointed Official Life Preserver Manufacturer for the society.

Did Eliza Stunt! Fell In

I never could swim, so one Sunady morning we tried to cross the ice by jumping from one cake of ice to the other—you know, the Eliza kind of stunt, I fell in, but Eddie Heinekes made it all right—an old schoolmate of mine, who is, or was, at the Courthouse until recently.—Edw. M. Scheid.

But No One Rescued "Cop" Who Fell In!

The canal boys were always ready to rescue somebody that fell in—except when it was the "cop."

Charles Peterson, Sr., 432 Park avenue, Aurora, Ind., writes that his most thrilling experience along the canal—and one of his happiest—was "when the 'cop' grabbed for me, but fell into the canal himself!"

He does not say that anybody went to the rescue of the "cop."

Welcome! Here's an Old Canal Boat Builder!

I surely can qualify as a member of Canal Swimmers' Society. Forty-two years ago I lived at Marshall and Canal. I built passenger and sand boats at this location. My recreation was swimming, fishing and shooting ducks in season. During winter I cut ice for slaughter houses and breweries.

BEN STAUB,
30 Conklin Street, City.

After Their Canal Play They Sold Times-Stars!

Mr. Charles Ludwig, Editor Canal Swimmers—Thousands of us readers enjoyed the Canal Swimmers' column. I with my brother almost lived in the canal, from early morning, in vacation time, until time to sell our Times-Stars. We also battled with the Mohawk crowd, or rather against them, and often were forced to find shelter in the sand-house, our fort.

In order to become a member of our bunch one was required to be able to throw across the canal. I remember distinctly when I was ineligible to membership because I was too small to do so, and how I practiced almost constantly until I was able to throw clear across.

"Sweet Adeline" and Old Lager on Cruise on Venetian Waters

I was a member of a club of boys on the bank of the canal and had a canoe, in which we made frequent trips up the canal. A number of times we took along an "eighth" of the good old stuff and some string instruments. We would paddle up the stream until the refreshments ran low and then drift slowly back home singing "Sweet Adeline" and all the old favorites. The canal had a quaint, romantic air at night and we imagined we were cruising the waters of Venice.

—Herman A. Krause, City.

GILMORE BOAT CLUB WAS FAMOUS FOR ITS CANAL REGATTAS AND OUTINGS—PHOTO FROM VAL KAISER.

There's the Canal, Boys! And No Glass or Tin! Just Pick Your Swimming Hole—Jump Right In!

Boys, there's the old canal on the next page—prepared once more for you by our artist, George Bristol. Just pick out your favorite swimming hole and take a last plunge!

The road is clear—no "cops" around—and if you prefer to take a high dive off one of the bridges, go right ahead. Plenty of canal boats passing, too, and if you want one more free ride, just hop on.

A few of the oldest old-timers will recall fishing and swimming in the Eggleston avenue section of the canal, where it joined the Ohio. Thousands will recall the Canal street section, and the stretch from the Plum street bend northward—the old City Hospital and Music Hall sites, the towpath to Mohawk and Brighton, then First Basin at Hopple street and Second Basin just beyond.

The map will bring back sweet memories to many who played around Fanning's Dry Dock and the pretty overflow falls of the canal at the foot of Clifton. And Mummert's Basin, Blair's Basin, the Mitchell avenue aqueduct, popular Ross Lake and the other basins will bring back happy recollections to great numbers of Canal Swimmers.

Speaker Nicholas Longworth of House of Representatives Was Canoeist and Swimmer

Speaker Nicholas Longworth of the House of Representatives was among the very first members of the Canal Swimmers' Society.

"I can easily qualify for membership," said Speaker Longworth. "When I was a boy my father was president of the Cincinnati Canoe Club on Ross Lake, some miles out of Cincinnati on the canal. On Saturday nights we would go there and swim and paddle our canoes around the lake almost the whole night through. Glad the Canal Swimmers' Society is bringing back those pleasant memories of boyhood times."

Declares Boulevard Should Bear Unique Name, Towpath

The boulevard should be named the Towpath, writes E. S. Howard, comptroller of the Young Men's Christian Association, Cincinnati, and he adds:

"Our swimming hole was at the old aqueduct, south of Hartwell. The structural work furnished several elevations from which we could dive.

"An event which occurred every year was the building of a scow or flatboat. It took the combined efforts of the whole neighborhood gang to calk and tar, and when finished to launch and christen the craft.

J. Stacy Hill and Chum Ran Away from Home Via Canal

Nearly everybody at the Chamber of Commerce and Cincinnati Club wanted to join the new society.

J. Stacy Hill said: "I'm glad to join this famous Canal Club—but the memories are not all angelic. The towpath was my boyhood playground, and at 14 my chum and I ran away from home—we tramped along the towpath out of the city. We were caught and sent home. Was I chastised? Well, it was almost impossible for me to sit down for two days."

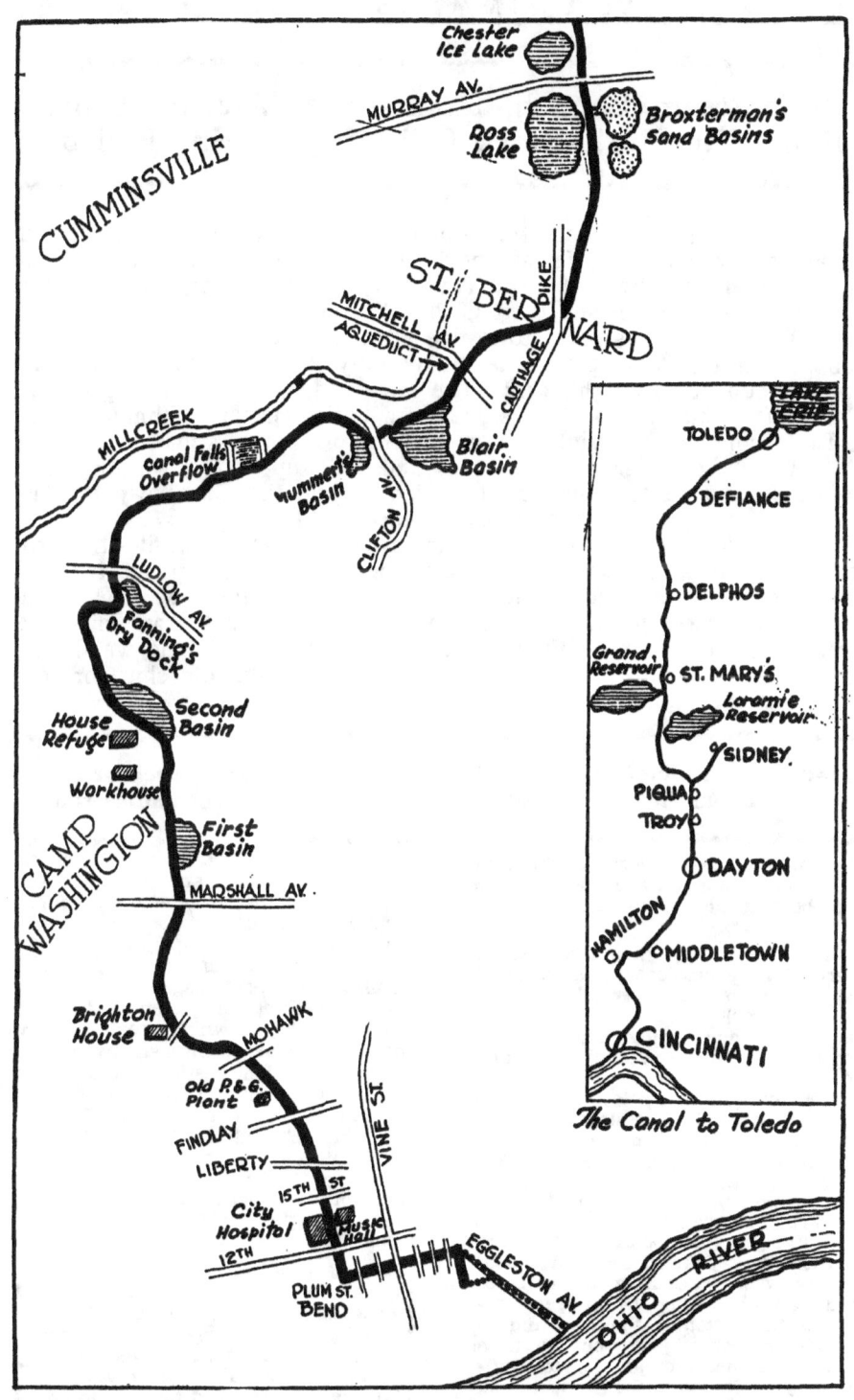

A CITY'S SWIMMING HOLE FOR A CENTURY—TEN MILES OF CANAL THROUGH CINCINNATI. PLAYGROUND FOR MANY THOUSANDS! PICK OUT YOUR FAVORITE POOLS, BOYS!

First Steam Launch, Homemade, Was a Misfit! Pump Too Big! Stack Fell Off! Engine Failed!

On another page is seen the famous Puritan Boat Club of 1884, with the first steam launch, so far as known, ever operated on the canal. The picture was loaned by Arthur A. Taylor, wholesale grocer, 2113 Central avenue, member of the old Boat Club, who said:

"This picture was taken forty-five years ago near Carthage when our club was on a Sunday spin in the canal's only steam launch of that time. In the group, left to right, are: The late Fred J. Mayer, vice president of the Fifth Third National Bank; Clifford Latta, Master Pohlman, Arthur A. Taylor and Samuel Winkler, now a New York business man.

"We built the launch ourselves and rode up and down the canal on many happy excursions, and I'm glad to join the Old Towpath Club now. My family lived near the canal since 1844.

"That first homemade steam launch of ours was a misfit—the propeller was too large and we lost one propeller. The pump was twice as big as needed. The smoke stack fell into the canal and I was elected to dive down and recapture it. Someone threw a cigar on the awning—and the awning burned up. Often the engine failed to work and we had to pull the boat home. But we had lots of fun on the old ship for four years, just the same."

Had Fun on Moerlein's Canal Picnic in 1888!

Conrad Richter, 70, "an old Brighton boy," brings back jolly memories of a canal boat picnic by Moerlein employes forty years ago.

"In the year 1888, when I worked at Moerlein's, the employes gave a canal boat picnic on a Sunday," he relates. "With the mules pulling us we started away from Findlay bridge about 9 a. m. with the Old Time Schnapps Band and enough room for some old Moerlein's. A number took fishing poles along. We started with music and singing, passed the rear part of St. Bernard graveyard and landed about a mile beyond. We had dancing, and quite often you would hear the words, "Let's have one!" Also, foot racing, baseball and swimming. No fishing! I guess the poles and lines are out there yet! Started for home about 5 in the evening. Coming in, Schnapps Band played and sang "Down Went McGinty to the Bottom of the Sea," and all the old-time songs. We went down to elbow and turned around back to Findlay bridge. Took out the empties, you know. Put them on towpath. It was all over. Some went to the brewery. I left, singing, for home."

Artist Painted Houseboat In Lovely Towpath Setting

Mat A. Daly, well-known Cincinnati artist, often painted and sketched along the canal in his early days and found inspiration in many of the country towpath scenes. In 1889 he painted the beautiful view, "Near Cumminsville," that is published on next page. The picture shows something rarely seen on the canal —a houseboat, in which people lived as they camped along the canal.

"I was an enthusiastic canal swimmer in my boyhood days, swam in every part of the canal from the old City Hospital to Lockland," said Mr. Daly. "Often on Saturdays and Sundays we would go out to one of the basins along the canal, camp out overnight and swim and fish to our hearts' content. Ah! Blissful memories!"

Rescued Three-Legged Dog!

I had a three-legged dog. He was thrown in the water and could not swim. I jumped in, clothes and all, rescued the dog and fought the boy that threw him in.—M. B. Sohmer.

"CANAL SHANTYBOAT"—SCENE NEAR CUMMINSVILLE—PAINTED BY MATT A. DALY, IN 1889.

"Cheese It! The Cop!" The Harrowing Cry! Canal Swimmers Grab Clothes! In Terror Fly!

"Cheese it! The cop's coming!"

This clarion cry, stirring and unforgettable, sent thrills through thousands of boys swimming in the canal without the legally required bathing clothes.

It put them to exciting flight, with "pants and shirt" under their arms.

For the boys did not want to be bothered with clothes when swimming—they preferred to be bothered by "the cops."

Indeed, the phrase, "Cheese it, the cop!" has been adopted as the official slogan and secret password of the Canal Swimmers' Society.

Fred D. Lohman, well-known artist, of 2609 Jefferson avenue, and a graduate Canal Swimmer, shows in his jolly cartoon on the next page how the pursued boys could run—and recalls many other canal episodes.

Nearly Drowned First Time Dove in Canal

My first experience in the canal nearly cost me my life. It happened at Canal and Fifteenth streets. My older brothers were in and I asked my mother if I could go in. She said yes, knowing my brothers could swim. I got out of my clothes in a jiffy and yelled "Here I come," and dove. I thought all you had to do was dive in and the rest was easy, but, oh, my, what a difference! They told me after it was all over, if it hadn't been for one of the boys seeing my hand and grabbing it, I'd have been surely drowned. So I guess I'm entitled to membership in your society. As a lad I often walked across the Walnut street bridge on the outside rail, it being only about two inches wide. It was a dangerous stunt.—Ferd. L. Ludwig, 416 East avenue, Hamilton, O.

Was Whipped Twice for Only One Swim! A Record!

W. H. Whiteford, 3214 Brookfield avenue, writes: "I swam in the canal once. I told my mother I was going in swimming. So she whipped me before I went. I sure enjoyed my swim. Thinking everything was all right I told her of the fun I had. So she whipped me again."

Saved After He Went Under Third Time

George M. Fitzpatrick, 4525 Lawrence street, St. Bernard: "I fell into the canal as a little boy and would have been drowned but for a pal we called Hicky Hacky, who saved my life by diving in after I had gone down the third time. Many a time I dove off the old mud digger that dug the mud from the canal and put it on boats to be taken away."

With Straws, Boys Syphoned Highwine From Barrels

Charles Rentrop, Sr., 110 Lyon street, tells how his gang used to syphon liquor from barrels on the canal:

"Caught two buffalo fish, 14½ and 15 pounds, in Seven Mile Basin. One dark night was sitting on the east side of Vine street bridge, heard a splash, ran under bridge and found a man's body—dead! Used to ride on boat called Trenton, which would bring in highwine—boys used to tap barrels and suck it out with straws, and oh, boy! you should have seen some of them. Saw dead body of man raised with a towline of a canal boat at Race street. When canal was let out we used to catch a tubful of catfish and sunfish."

"AIN'T WE GOT FUN!"—DRAWN BY F. D. LOHMAN.

Canal Boats Carried Ice to Town Before Ice-Motors Won Renown

The picture of the well-known old canal boat "Robert R. Reynolds," kindly loaned by Henry J. Newton, and published on the opposite page, is doubly interesting, for it shows, in its background, the great exposition building erected over the canal for the Centennial Exposition of 1888. This building, called Machinery Hall, was the longest show building ever erected in the history of Cincinnati.

The picture was taken forty-one years ago. The man with the ice tongs is Henry J. Newton, 226 West Sixty-ninth street, Carthage. The man with the broom is William Barclif and the woman is Barclif's mother. The mother, with her son, ran the boat after her husband died, Newton writes. The little dog on the front deck was the pet of all the boatmen.

In the old days the ice boats brought great harvests of ice to Cincinnati from the ice basins, fed by the canal waters, a few miles above the city.

Set Canal Afire

I think I am the only person who ever set the canal on fire. Years ago, while playing along its banks at Hartwell, the canal was covered with an oil which we discovered was inflammable. We used it in making our bonfires on the bank, and I went a little further and threw a lighted piece of wood into the stream, which burned for quite a while on the water.—Clark Stagman, assistant treasurer Western and Southern Life Insurance Company.

Had War Dance!

Sixty years ago at Brighton the gang would call out, "One, two three!" and the whole bunch would jump in the canal with clothes on and swim all the afternoon to our hearts' content, then when swimming time was up we would get together and go to the top of Fairview Heights, undress, wring out our clothes, lay them out for the sun to dry and jollify by having an Indian war dance while waiting for the clothes to dry.—Frank W. Tech.

Governor Cooper Joins Club As "Official Diving Board Provider"

"I am happy to join the Canal Swimmers' Society," is the message from Myers Y. Cooper, governor of Ohio. "I hope I may be admitted under the classification of Canal Builder.

"I built half a dozen houses along the canal at Dixmyth avenue and often saw the placid old stream and have many recollections about it.

"The canal was so picturesque that its memory should be carried down to future generations. May the grand deeds of the Canal Swimmers never be forgotten!

"If the classification of Canal Builder is no longer open in your society, perhaps I may be admitted as Diving Board Provider, for many a canal diver leaped in from my boards."

ICEBOAT AND CREW, 1888; MACHINERY HALL OF EXPOSITION IN REAR—PHOTO FROM HENRY J. NEWTON.

"The Good Old Days" Were Days of Bliss For Thousands of Happy Groups Like This!

See the happy group of towpath playmates on the next page!

No doubt you recall a similar group to which you once belonged and the

> Sweet childish days, that were as long
> As twenty days are now.

The picture sent in by Frank J. Meder, Jr., 1749 North Bend road, College Hill, was taken in 1901. It brings back the poet's lines:

> I remember, I remember,
>   How my childhood fleeted by—
> The mirth of its December,
>   And the warmth of its July.

Days of mirth and innocence, when "life went a-Maying, with Nature, Hope and Poesy!"

Seen in the group of children are Harry, Fred and Walter Breuer, Frank Meder, John Stuebber and sister, Clifford Keller and sister, William Schwaegelie and several others.

It was of another group of playing youths that Gray wrote his famous lines:

> Yet, ah! Why should they know their fate,
> Since sorrow never comes too late,
> And happiness too swiftly flies?
> Thought would destroy their paradise.
> No more;—where ignorance is bliss,
>   'Tis folly to be wise.

And yet the Canal Scribe ventures to hope that fate has dealt kindly with all the towpath playmates.

Pleasant Memories of the Towpath Are Recalled

Charles P. Taft, publisher of the Times-Star, recalled delightful towpath days.

The publication in the Times-Star, in September, 1928, of the scenes along the old canal, the views of the canal boats, of boys swimming in the placid stream and playing along the towpath, brought back to him happy memories of his childhood.

"I think I'm eligible to join the Canal Swimmers' Society, too," he said with a laugh, "for as a boy I used to swim in the old canal in the basin out at Clifton." And Mrs. Taft also has pleasant memories of a playday along the Old Towpath when she joined with friends on a ride into the country on one of the canal boat excursions.

HAPPY, CAREFREE TOWPATH PLAYMATES OF 1901, GATHERED ON BANK OF CANAL—PHOTO FROM F. J. MEDER, JR.

In Bitter Cold of '84 Firemen Fought Mighty Conflagration in Soap Factory on Towpath

January 7, 1884, was one of the most thrilling days along the old canal—the day of the great Procter & Gamble soap factory fire. Many recall the day.

The plant had been on the canal at Charlotte street, north of Findlay, since 1837, and was referred to in the newspapers describing the fire as "the largest soap factory in the world," with over 500 employes.

The fire broke out at 1 p. m. and spread rapidly through many buildings.

An electric alarm notified all the employes of the fire and they were able to make their escape—but many returned to carry out candles and other supplies. A general alarm was turned in and soon a score of engines were pouring water on the flames—many of the engines pumping from the canal. The day was bitter cold and the fire fighters were soon covered with ice.

"At 2:30 p. m. the fire reached the underground oil cellars and there was an explosion, followed by great black fumes," said one account. "At 3:30 the fire burst through the candle factory into the south soap factory. The entire building was saturated with grease and oil and the sight at the time the main building was ablaze was indeed a grand one.

"A little later the heavy walls of the soap factory fell with a tremendous crash, after which a flood of flames leaped forth and seemed to lick the very skies. During the fire employes carried candles and other supplies from the buildings and William Dukes fell from a second story and was seriously injured.

"The oil factory, candle wareroom, south soap factory, candle factory, melting house and press house were destroyed, with a loss estimated at $250,000. The new north soap factory was not burned."

Ruins Were Picturesque

And there is the human touch. "When the flames were at their height James Gamble left his own property to care for the firemen, who were suffering from the intense cold," wrote one scribe. "He telephoned to a downtown restaurant for forty gallons of coffee, but when the answer came that so large an amount could not be furnished, Mr. Gamble bought coffee pots and tin cups and personally attended to the distribution of over fifty gallons of coffee and hundreds of sandwiches."

It is recorded that John Hauck, the brewer, was also on the scene, and "gave the firemen and policemen a warm supper."

The fire burned through the night and the loss was estimated at $250,000. Fire Chief Bunker and his men were covered with ice and some of the firemen had to be taken away and "thawed out."

The ruins made an unusually picturesque scene that attracted large crowds. The gaunt walls were covered with heavy ice, and icicles ten to thirty feet long hung from the telegraph poles.

PRETTY, RUSTIC CANAL SCENE: THE LOCKS AT LOCKLAND—PHOTO BY FRANK WILMES.

Gay Gondoliers in 1888 Centennial Exposition Hall Over Canal—Structure Quarter Mile Long

On an adjoining page you will observe a picture of the famous Machinery Hall, built right over the top of the canal for the Cincinnati Centennial Exposition of 1888. This was one of the longest buildings ever erected here—its length was 1,248 feet!

Machinery Hall was erected in the rear of Music Hall, on Plum street, and, nearly a quarter of a mile long, extended from Twelfth street on the south to Fifteenth street on the north.

The canal ran through the middle of the building and was alive with gondolas and gondoliers, that were a part of the exposition entertainment. The building was 114 feet wide at the ends and 150 feet wide in the center where it connected with Music Hall.

The aisles on each side of the canal, in the building, were devoted to exhibits of machinery. There were attractive pavilions at the north and south ends of the great structure—and also a refreshment hall. Four bridges, inside the building, crossed the canal, which presented a charming Venetian picture. Arches, reaching forty feet above the water, formed the dome-like roof. The building exposition authorities proudly announced that the building was illuminated at night "by innumerable jets of gas and electric lights," and that the views presented in the building "are something entirely unique." James W. McLaughlin, Cincinnati, was the architect.

The great centennial exposition included elaborate exhibits in Music Hall and in the special buildings in Washington Park, as well as notable Government displays by the War, Navy, Interior and Agricultural Departments, United States Museum and United States Fish Commission.

James Allison was president of the centennial and the commissioners were Lee H. Brooks, Henry S. Snider, L. H. McCammon, E. O. Eshelby, M. E. Kuhn, May Fechheimer, Augustus Honshell, George Kerper, J. M. Blair, John Goetz, George A. Gray, P. G. March, A. B. Champion and Levi C. Goodale, the latter president of the Chamber of Commerce. Perhaps Mr. Goodale is the only one of the group surviving—and he is a member of the Canal Club! Amor Smith was then Mayor.

Frank M. Biddle, minister of the Fairmount Christian Church, tells how he took 300 boys from the House of Refuge on a canal boat to the great exposition hall over the canal in 1888.

"Forty years ago," he writes, "I enjoyed a most delightful ride on its placid waters. At that time I was military instructor for the Cincinnati House of Refuge, visiting it several afternoons a week to drill the boys.

"On September 27, 1888, the children of the refuge, having been invited to attend one of our famous expositions, 300 boys and girls, in charge of Assistant Superintendent Costello and myself, embarked on board a large canal boat with its prow turned toward Music Hall, my wife and others accompanying us. With laughter and song we glided along, while the mules pulled hard on the tow rope.

"The canal had been roofed in the rear of Music Hall, and a Venetian scene cleverly reproduced, with gay gondoliers guiding their boats. With flags flying, the fine House of Refuge Drum Corps led us from our boat into Music Hall, where I took command of the four companies of boys and entertained the audience that packed every inch of space with wonderful exhibition drills and a dress parade on the stage. After the children were treated to pop corn and decorated with medals, we all marched on board our chartered canal boat and headed for home."

MACHINERY HALL, 1,250 FEET LONG, OVER CANAL—CENTENNIAL EXPOSITION, 1888. SEE GONDOLAS!

Our Mayor, a Lawyer, Joins Club By a Ruse!
"Friend's Dog Swam"—So He's In, and No Dues!

Mayor Murray Seasongood was among the first to apply for membership in the Canal Club and was pleased to recall memories of his boyhood days along the canal.

"I never swam in the canal—but I wonder if I am entitled to join the Canal Society because of the fact that my friend, Dr. Louis Ransohoff, had a pet dog that swam in the canal every day," said the mayor. "We used to like to watch him swim in the not too immaculate waters. I lived on Garfield place and Ransohoff and I attended the Tenth District School, located on the canal bank. So the canal was a happy and familiar playground for us, and I often skated upon it, and once fell into the water."

The fact that the mayor skated on and played along the canal entitles him to charter membership in the society—and even without that experience, he would be admitted, because his friend's dog swam in the canal. This automatically makes Dr. Ransohoff a member also.

"I certainly have had a lot of fun out of the canal stories in the Times-Star," Mayor Seasongood said, "and a great many people have spoken to me about this quaint and interesting Canal Swimmers' Society that brings back such delightful old memories."

Boy Hero Decorated With G. A. R. Badge

The only boy lifesaver ever decorated for bravery by the child he saved from drowning in the canal was the lad who rescued Donald Copelan, son of Police Chief William Copelan.

Robert Copelan, another son, told the story after joining the Canal Swimmers' Club:

"I often swam in the canal, but my brother Donald, aged 6, had a close call. He fell into the water and a larger boy, whose name I do not know, jumped in and saved him. Donald was grateful for the boy's brave action and thought he ought to be rewarded and decorated for bravery. So Donald came home, took my mother's badge of membership in the auxiliary of the Grand Army of the Republic, Israel Ludlow Corps, and pinned it on the breast of his rescuer.

"Mother looked everywhere for her lost badge—and only long afterward did she find out what became of it."

School Is Burning! So Let's All Go Skating

When the Third Intermediate School had a fire upon a zero day, classes were dismissed and so the gang went skating to Second Basin, back of the workhouse.

We swam in canal in back of Vine Street Cemetery. The boys used to jump the sand floats when they passed the bridges from the top of the bridge, and then when the boat would come into the side of the shore, making the turn, would hop off again. My companions were Charles Stammel, surgeon United States Army; Ferd Zuenkeler, the Geiger boys of Elm Street Club fame, Dr. Ed Enz, and many more.—George F. Kreh, secretary, George H. Ward Paper Company.

From Hollywood

Well do I remember the canal-boys diving off bridges and looking like frogs, with their legs spread out—the pretty curtains of the canal boat windows—the ice-boats—Greenwood Foundry, and all the rest—Victoria Borkosky, 6331 Lexington avenue, Hollywood, Cal.

Oh, the Dances and Feasts in Bellevue House! Now All Is Vanished! Remains But a Mouse!

BELLEVUE HOUSE—PHOTO LOANED BY C. F. HUSS

Gaze once more on the beautiful and famous old Bellevue House, that was one of Cincinnati's most popular recreation resorts during the '80s and early '90s.

It stood out boldly, on a picturesque promontory, at the summit of Bellevue Hill, just to the east of the canal and at the top of the Elm street incline—but has long since been torn down.

"Bellevue House, leased by the Windisch-Muhlhauser Brewing Company, was one of the four leading hilltop resorts of the old days," said Charles F. Windisch, president of the company that has been located on the canal for sixty years. "Lookout House on Jackson Hill, the Highland House on Mt. Adams, and the Price Hill House were the other three."

Joseph Uhl, bookkeeper of the brewing company for the past fifty-eight years, said: "As I recall it, Bellevue House was built in the later '70s by members of the Banner Packing Company, who leased it to the old street railway company of which John Kilgour, father of Bayard Kilgour, was the head. The Windisch-Muhlhauser

Company leased it for fifteen years from the street railway, and throughout the '80s the Bellevue House was a great hilltop resort.

"It was a great and striking looking building, perched on its pretty hilltop. In the basement was the kitchen. On the first floor was the grand concert hall, with tables for dining. Concerts were given by the finest bands, playing the best of music. Along almost the entire north side of this hall was a long bar with a foot rail—one of the longest in the city—and it was often packed with people. On the second floor was a fine dance floor and ballroom, rented to clubs and societies for dances and balls and many memorable events were given. There were broad porches around the building for fresh air and a wonderful sight of the city below.

"On the hillside, in the open, was a huge platform with tables and chairs, and a thousand people could sit there and look down upon the remarkable city panorama in the valley.

"There were gardens, too, and in the rear a large dancing pavilion. On Sundays and holidays we would sell more than a hundred kegs of beer. Great crowds came up the incline. But the Sunday closing law spelled the doom of Bellevue House—and it closed in the early '90s, I think, and has since been torn down."

"And don't forget the roller-coaster they had on the hillside around Bellevue House," added Ye Kentucky Editor, Harry Meier, "and the bowling alleys with balls that had no finger holes, and the wonderful fireworks displays there on the Fourth of July, and the big cannon fired off about 4 a. m. on the Fourth from Bellevue House and that awoke the whole neighborhood for an early start."

As a child this writer, too, played around Bellevue House in its fading glory. Now all has vanished, except perhaps a little mouse down in the foundation ruins.

Indiana Heard From!

We want to join the Canal Society. We were born and raised in Cincinnati and our place on the old canal was at Brighton, and during vacation it was morning, afternoon and night to take our swim in the canal. It did not take long to undress, as all we had on was a pair of pants and shirt and a 10-cent straw hat. Those were certainly great days. We can see the gilded cow on top of the old Brighton Hotel. Trusty prisoners released from the workhouse and coming back to town on the towpath would grab us and throw us in the canal, clothes and all.—Will and Ed Tech, North Vernon, Ind.

Made Mighty Catches With One-Cent Fish Pole

Born in 1855, I lived around Mohawk as a boy. I had all the pleasures any boy could have on the old canal, boating, fishing, swimming, skating, cutting ice for the butchers. Whenever I wanted to eat some nice fresh fish for breakfast I would get up in the morning early, about daybreak, and with a can of worms and a one-cent pole catch all the fish we could eat in about an hour and they were some fish, nice yellow cat and often channel cat.—J. G. Linser, Sr., 612 Third avenue, Dayton, Ky.

When Canal Boat Was Changed Into a Saloon

George F. Kinzel, Howard Apartments, St. Leger place, Walnut Hills, writes:

"I also recall when Robinson's Circus came from their winter quarters at John and Poplar streets and would open the circus season at the circus lot where now stands our Music Hall.

"During vacation time I went with my uncle, Lafe Kinzel, who was captain of the canal boat called Thomas Morgan. I recall one summer when they had a saengerfest in the old Music Hall my uncle rigged up a canal boat as a saloon. The boat had two compartments and he had awnings stretched from bow to stern and steps leading up from shore the entire length of the boat and tables and benches aside of midship. People came out of rear entrance of Music Hall, mounted steps to boat and sat down and drank beer and ate lunch and had a good time.

Welcome News of Last Canal Boat

I drove down to Fourteenth and Plum with the last boatload of sand with four mules from Fred J. Broxterman's sand pit. Now you can see the old boat at the pit in Bond Hill, where there is still water in the canal.—John K. Kushman.

Pioneer Steam Launch Took Many Happy Parties On Outings Along the Towpath.

WEEK-END SPIN ON CANAL—PHOTO FROM GEORGE LIPPOLD.

"Yes, sir, we took many an outing in our canal launches, starting Saturday evening, camping out and returning Sunday, and had plenty to eat and drink—and the whole cost to each of us was only about fifty cents," said George Lippold, 2428 Halstead street, who contributed the above picture.

"My launch was named the Olympia, in honor of Dewey's flagship, for he had just won the battle of Manila. The launch shown above was built in 1888 by the late Fred Wm. Hempelman and his sons, Edward, 2408 Central Parkway, William and George, pioneer canal craft builders, and took out many happy parties."

Fumes of Alcohol!

Earl Butler said: "We used to smell the alcohol fumes from the empty barrels at the Clifton Springs Distillery—and would become quite dizzy from them. We also used to take the paraffin out of the canal boats and chew it for chewing gum."

Baked Potatoes and Fish!

Dear Mr. Ludwig: Reading about the Canal Swimmers puts me in mind of the days when the boys in the neighborhood would meet on Vine street and have baked potatoes and fish on the canal bank at night. Those were happy days.
—W. C. (Smiley) Frey.

"V," Mystic Towpath Symbol, Meant: "We're Going Swimming"

Peter J. Faulkner joined the club and, being duly sworn, testified as follows:

Gee, what memories the forming of the Towpath Club brings of boyhood's happy days spent on the "raging canal."

Our gang's favorite swimming hole was the Cheapside Basin, just south of Court street. Every evening at sundown the boys would foregather when the leader went around with two fingers stuck up in the shape of a V. The mystic signal (only understood by the boys) meant a rush to the old canal and a dip in its tawny water, in our one-piece bathing suits.

Jack Kearns stepped on a jagged piece of glass and we boys thought he was going to die immediately. When we saw the blood spurting from the wound, we all formed a circle around him and started a prayer for the good of his soul; but were interrupted by the harsh command of our leader, Jimmie Doyle, to tear up our waists and bind up the wound.

Other halcyon days were spent in boating, fishing and skating on the dear old stream.

During the Court House riots, a barricade was thrown up on the south side of the canal, guarding the bridge approaches at Sycamore, Main and Walnut, and soldiers manned them with Gatling guns and Springfield rifles, holding the mob to the north side of the canal way.

On Sunday morning following the destruction by fire of the Court House, a youth ventured across the Main street bridge in defiance of the command to halt by the soldiers, and I saw him fall, pierced by a rifle bullet from the barricade.

At Court and Main was a general store where long bamboo fishing poles, bait and skiffs could be had, the latter for 15 cents per hour.

Farther down Eggleston avenue I used to watch men skimming the grease off the water as it flowed from the candle factories, and then later on see them sell the grease to the same factories from which it came. And I saw the ice cutters sawing great blocks of ice and storing it in the numerous ice houses along its banks.

Bridwell Visioned Parkway Down to Its Details in 1898

Harry Mullane Bridwell, advertising designer, 606 Second National Bank Building, sends a drawing of the canal boulevard as visioned thirty years ago by his father, H. L. Bridwell. It's like a dream come true! It shows a subway, with electrically driven cars, and on the surface a fine boulevard, with trees and parkway just as you see it today.

The Times-Star printed Bridwell's plans in 1898 and said of them:

"From Broadway to Brighton this subway is to be arched over and an asphalt avenue constructed above, occupying the whole width of the canal property and having through the middle a chain of small parks which mask the openings into the subway." And that is what we have today!

He Didn't Get the Promised Spanking

My most thrilling experience was to have a "cop" swipe my clothes and take them to the police station up on McMicken and Walnut streets. It was a sad predicament. I had to send my cousin, Elmer Prell, of Milton street, to my home for more clothes, and then take my mother with me to get my other clothes back. They (the clothes) were returned, on my mother's promise to the "cops" that I be given a spanking and made stay away from the canal.

You can imagine how long I kept out of the "old swimmin' hole"—and I didn't get the lickin', either.—John A. Prell, 3802 Park avenue, Latonia Station, Covington, Ky.

> See the Ice on Double-Header! Keg on Top of Keg!
> What a Menu: Catfish, Turtle and Frog-Leg!

OUTING AT LOCKLAND LOCKS—PHOTO FROM GEORGE LIPPOLD.

"This was one of our famous canal outings of 1898," said George Lippold, at the George F. Otte Company. "Those were surely the happy days. Our crowd from Brighton—or Mosquitoville, as they called our neighborhood on the canal, because the marshy district bred such huge mosquitoes—went out to a nice place at the Lockland locks on Decoration Day, 1898.

"Of course, we had a band of music, and baseball bats and gloves. We bought several 'eighths' at the brewery for seventy-five cents each. Our launch was so arranged that we could fill the entire sides with bottles!

"We would catch turtles, frogs and catfish—the sweetest catfish—and turtles that weighed ten to twelve pounds. I was the champion frog-catcher—caught great big ones with a lamp for Mr. Fey, then in the wine business. The turtles were plentiful around the timbers of sunken old canal boats.

In the group above—the type foundry crowd—are Charles Anstead, Charles Bloebaum, Al Bauer, Frank Magley, Otto Wagner, Ed Bender, Jacob Nessler, my brothers William and John, and myself."

Caught Biggest Fish!

Dr. A. J. Bauman, Erie and Edwards Road—About twenty-five years ago I caught a fish that weighed fourteen pounds in the old canal. I think that was the record catch then.

M-m-m—The Good Apples!

We had a special swimming place about a half mile east of the waterfalls which we called the Willows. After swimming we would fill ourselves on apples which we would get near this swimming hole.—Jacob Staigle.

"WE LOST TWO MEN"

Abe Fletcher writes: "Dear Ludwig—Your beautiful poem, 'We Lost Two Men,' with its thrilling water scene, that was read in the U. S. Congress, deserves a place in the Canal Book. Capt. Fried of the steamer Roosevelt, describing the rescue of the crew of the sinking freighter Antinoe in a terrific gale, with waves 60 feet high, wirelessed: 'We lost two men, Wirtanan and Heitman, who volunteered to row a lifeboat through the terrific gale. But a great wave engulfed them. We lost four other lifeboats but finally saved the Antinoe crew.'"

"WE LOST TWO MEN"
By Charles Ludwig

There's so much work to do today,
And so much golf and bridge to play,
A million cars to whirl away,
We have no time to mourn or pray—
    When heroes die.

A howling storm, a raging sea,
A sinking hulk upon the lee,
A slashing blizzard, roaring gale,
And shattered decks and tattered sail.

Who'll row a lifeboat through that hell
With death a-riding every swell?
Who'll risk his hide to save the tars
Still clinging vain to crashing spars?

Two dauntless sailors volunteer—
No football crowd to rise and cheer.
Through hissing waters, shrieking skies,
They fight the tempest of their lives.

They battle on, near reach the goal,
As wilder yet the billows roll;
Now sweeps a giant, angry wave,
A yawning maw—it is their grave.

"We lost two men"—terse ship report.
Thank God, in times of sheik and sport
The tribe's still true. A wreath to them,
These gallant dead—we lost two MEN!

Though there's much work to do today,
And so much golf and bridge to play,
A million cars to whisk away,
Let's pause a moment, just to say,
    We lost two MEN.

Squadron Pretty and Bright! Canoes All Painted White!

The White Squadron Canoe Club had three canoes, painted white, and one admiral.

"We kept our canoes in a cellar at Eighth and Race streets, near where we lived, and Saturday afternoons carried them to the canal," said M. E. Remelin, membership secretary of the Chamber of Commerce.

"We paddled for two hours, out to the Bond Hill basin, opposite Ross Lake, camped out all night, swam, boated and fished. At places the water was sixty feet deep, so we understood. We took lunch and skillets along and cooked meals, too. We had a regular night watch, to keep tramps from taking our canoes. Sunday evening we paddled back home.

"We were about fifteen years old—that was in 1886—and our group included Allie Ware, who was the admiral; Will Brickel, George Coleman, Clint McCord, Billy Heberle and others. Ah, those were days of perfect bliss!"

Years ago a policeman swung his cane at my friend, Fatty Weiss, who ducked the blow—while the tremendous swing unbalanced the "cop" and he fell into the canal.—H. G. Knodel.

An old woman, employed in a rag shop at Jackson street, leaped from the second story during a big fire there and was killed.—Elizabeth and John Braegger.

Edward Nurre, picture frame manufacturer, saw one boy electrocuted on the electric mule and another dive to his death from the top of the Fourteenth street bridge—his head striking a rock. A fireman was killed in a fire at the Nurre plant on the canal.

Capt. Eugene Y. Handlan, aged 89, perhaps the oldest surviving Ohio River captain of this section, and who served as ensign commanding on the Mississippi and other Southern waters during the Civil War, is a graduate of the old canal.

He learned his first lessons in navigation on its clear waters eighty years ago.

"I lived in Camp Washington as a boy and away back in the '40's—eighty years ago, when I was not yet ten—I played along the canal in that district and became a lover of the water," said the venerable old captain, still hale and hearty, despite his years.

WHEN CANAL "BURNED," CARTHAGE AQUEDUCT FELL AFTER FIRE, RELEASING FLOOD—PHOTO BY W. H. BOONE.

Mr. Rembold, When a Boy, Fell Into Canal In His New Suit

C. H. Rembold, general manager of the Times-Star, is one of the large number of Cincinnatians who can qualify for membership in the Towpath Club because they fell into the waters of the canal in their boyhood days.

And, as in so many other cases, young Rembold was wearing a brand new suit when the accident occurred, and this added vastly to the significance of the affair.

It was more than fifty-eight years ago that Mr. Rembold and two boy friends were riding in a double-bowed skiff at second basin, opposite the workhouse. The oarsman, in the middle, splashed water on the lads at the ends. Young Rembold offered to do the rowing. The oarsman agreed, and arose and so did Rembold, and as the two tried to exchange places and pass each other, the boat tipped and both were thrown into the water. They scrambled to the shore and dried their clothing.

Mr. Rembold was interested in the announcement that James N. Gamble "swam in the canal over seventy-five years ago, and worked on its banks in the Procter & Gamble soap factory," and had been named honorary president of the Canal Swimmers' Society.

"Around 1874 I lived near the Mohawk section of the canal, and I know that Mr. Gamble really worked in the soap factory," said Mr. Rembold. "Many a time I saw him working in overalls! He was factory superintendent for years and was not afraid of work!"

Judge Goebel Fried Fish!

"My memories of the canal date back over seventy years," said Judge and Former Congressman Herman P. Goebel. "I was raised Over-the-Rhine—lived at Race and Findlay streets. When I was a child my brother took me into the canal to show me how to swim. He let me go in the middle and told me to swim. I sank and thought I was going to be drowned—but he pulled me out.

"Later we boys went in swimming every summer night—the canal water was clean in those early days. Sometimes I fished in it, caught a string of small fish and fried them at home.

"At times the canal would be filled with boys swimming, and suddenly one would shout:

"'The cops are coming!'

"There would be a grand scramble to get out of the water and escape with clothing under arms.

"The policemen would catch a bunch of us and march us two by two up the street in front of our homes as punishment—and then release us."

Great Picnic, But Canal Went Dry and Boat Stuck in Mud!

Shortly after the George H. Thomas Post, G. A. R., organized its drum corps in 1886, the committee in charge of us youngsters hired a canal boat and with our fifes and drums took us for a ride up toward Lockland. About noon the water was let out of the canal and we were stuck in the mud until the next day.—Louis Swikert, 4315 Ridgeview.

Hurrah! We're Off on Picnic! On Boat Drawn by Six Mules!

I would dive from the towpath and stay under water until I reached the other shore. I also went to picnics at Ross Lake in Frank Lawrence's picnic boat, which was decorated in the National colors and drawn by six mules.—John Fasold, 5215 Roanoke.

ALONG SYLVAN TOWPATH AT CLIFTON—W. H. BOONE PHOTO.

Did Not Drown Kittens, But Got the Five Cents

It was my duty around the Brighton neighborhood to drown litters of kittens and pups in the canal, for which I received five cents, but as they scratched me I let them go before getting to the banks and spent the money in the candy store where now stands the Brighton Bank Building.

Having been in the Seventy-ninth Ohio Legislature at the time when our canal proposition came up, I put in many a hard hour of work explaining our situation in Cincinnati and why we wanted to change the canal to a boulevard.—Carl F. H. Krug, Krug Realty Company.

Old "Times" Newsboy Saw Canal Circus

Sol J. Levi, 1611 Union Trust Building, says: "In the '70s, when I was a newsboy and sold the old Cincinnati Times, predecessor of the Times-Star of today, I went on a picnic given by Col. R. M. Moore, who served as mayor of the city for some years. He was a great friend of the newsboys and gave the picnic for their benefit. We had a grand time. I often swam in the canal.

"Long ago there was a circus boat operating on the canal. It was kept by the famous old clown, Mike Lipman, and he and his family lived on the boat with his animals—dogs, monkeys, etc."

James N. Gamble, 93, President Emeritus of Society, Swam in Canal Over 80 Years Ago

James N. Gamble, the 93-year-old president emeritus of the Canal Swimmers' Society, and Cincinnati's beloved old patriarch, still writes his name with a firm, strong hand.

We have received a letter from Mr. Gamble in which he states that he appreciates the honor conferred upon him in naming him president emeritus of the Canal Swimmers' Society.

Mr. Gamble swam in the canal as a lad over eighty years ago and for years worked on the canal as superintendent of the old Procter & Gamble soap factory, on the towpath above Findlay street. He was a real, working superintendent—in boots and overalls and not afraid of old-fashioned toil. Today, at 93, he is a remarkable specimen of physical and mental manhood, a tall figure, hale and hearty, keenly interested in every civic and humanitarian project. As he motors now over the fine Towpath Boulevard he recalls happy days spent in the water there away back in the 1840's, when he and the canal, too, were young. He writes to the Canal Scribe:

Dear Mr. Ludwig:

I was preparing a communication addressed to your organization asking for admission into the membership of the Canal Swimmers' Club when my attention was called to the announcement already made that you had honored me by appointing me president emeritus.

I had as a young boy very interesting times swimming in the canal, as I lived on York street between Western row (Central avenue) and John street, and went to the canal, usually near the Mohawk Bridge. Later on, however, the activities were much greater and I had pleasant times swimming, boating and skating on the old canal.

I greatly appreciate the honor you have conferred upon me and desire to express my appreciation to you and accept it with thanks. I am sure that your unique undertaking will be interesting to those directly connected with it and to our city in general. I am, with kind regards,

Yours sincerely, JAMES N. GAMBLE.

Dove Under Boat! Was Caught on Nail!

Here was one time when a poor and ragged pair of pants were a life saver. A crowd of us boys were swimming, trying to outdo each other in daring. A mule-drawn canal boat was slowly passing. I, standing at the edge of the bank, dared the others to follow me and dived under the boat, but while passing under the keel my pants caught on a nail. Thanks to a kind Providence and a ragged pair of pants my struggles soon pulled me loose and I came up O K on the other side, a hero to the other kids but very tame in my own heart.—O. M. Gray.

"Teacher's Rattan," or "A Canal Boy's Lament"

Joe McCann, 2440 Williams avenue, Norwood, sends this:

"Years ago, when attending school on Mound street, my teacher, Miss Applegate, sent me up Western Row, now Central avenue, to buy a rattan for her so she could chastise some pupils. I played on the way for two hours—at the Plum street elbow of the canal—and when I got back to the school I was the first to be punished with that stick, for staying too long on the errand!

"In later years I worked on putting in hydraulic plants for Bowler, Henry Probasco and others, to pump water to their estates."

SPEEDING SOUTH OF MOHAWK AT FOUR MILES AN HOUR THIRTY YEARS AGO—PHOTO BY FRANK WILMES.

> **See the Thrilling Towpath Sight!**
> **How Bravely Do the Canal Boys Fight!**

Shouts of battle rent the air again today along the usually placid banks of the old canal!

The historic feud between the Mohawk and Liberty street gangs was resumed with the fury of Gettysburg!

Consternation reigned in the upper reaches of the Towpath!

Excited mothers, looking out of the fourth stories of their homes, prayed that their dear little Johnnies would escape with life and limb from the furious melee below.

It all started when Chick Bates innocently pulled his play wagon, with his little brother as passenger, along the Towpath toward the ice house, where he hoped to capture a load of ice, when no one was looking.

Butch Goots, who had jumped on a canal boat from a bridge, threw a rope around Chick's head as the boat passed him—and pulled Chick, his wagon and his little brother in the canal. Then the fight was on!

Hicks Eckert, famous for his daring, leaped right in and saved Chick's little brother from drowning, then swam out to the canal boat, climbed up the rudder, fought Butch and rolled him into the canal.

Butch ran north to call his gang—the other boys south to call theirs.

The Clans Gather

In a few minutes there was a mighty gathering of the clans. The Mohawks brought their front line into action armed with sling-shots. The Liberty street gang sent its shock troops forward with armfuls and pocketfuls of "sailers"—thin stones that sailed easily through the air.

The Mohawks got reinforcements from the hillside. A bunch of Bethlehemers came into the fray armed with a unique sort of catapult—weed-sticks on the end of which they placed lumps of clay that shot off when the sticks were whipped in the direction of the enemy.

There was charging to and fro—windows and gas-lamps along the canal succumbing to the attacks, and an occasional injured warrior limping off the battlefield back to mother—for worse punishment.

The alert Liberty street reserve forces made piles of stones at strategic places for use in emergency—and surprised the onrushing horde, whose supply was giving out. This was a trick of Gen. Joe Heintzman, who always studied Napoleon.

As a last resort the Mohawk leader used up a pocketful of trilobites—treasures of geology he had just gathered on Bellevue hill. The Liberty gang caught one of the enemy and plastered his hair full of stickers and burrs picked in big handfuls from weeds.

The police restored order—and the battle was a draw.

Yes, the fight is over—it was over thirty, fifty years ago. It's but a dream now—but man is such a belligerent animal, he loves even to recall the play battles of his youth.

Ten thousand Cincinnatians of today had these gang "debates" of yesterday—and they were a vital part of life along the old canal.

But the Mohawk and Liberty street and Brighton boys and the rest at last have formed a truce!

THIS WAS A FAVORITE SWIMMING HOLE—MITCHELL AVENUE AQUEDUCT. PHOTO BY W. H. BOONE.

When Canal Really Raged! Blizzard! Whew! Gale Stopped Boats! How It "Blew and Snew!"

You may laugh all you please about the "raging" canal, but—

On January 31, 1889, that placid old stream just reared up on its hind feet like a cantankerous old canal-mule and put on a paroxysm of rage the like of which was never seen before—or after.

Leading Cincinnatians, already anxious to have the canal replaced by a boulevard, took the Legislative Committee on Public Works, Columbus, on an excursion on the canal to show them the advisability of abolishing the old stream.

They went on the canalboat Bavaria, specially fitted up for the excursion. But the canal did not wish to carry its would-be executioners.

It began to rage, and kick, and foam at the mouth.

A terrific blizzard arose!

Snow and sleet swept the decks!

A veritable hurricane blew through the cabins of the crew—and the delegation of State officials and local dignitaries and business men, who had to stand on the open deck, had no protection whatever!

GALE ON CANAL

They built four charcoal fires—but the gale blew harder and harder.

The canvas roof-covering was as nothing.

The wind beat against the legislators and chilled them to the bone!

Half frozen, they surrendered! They gave up the canal trip as a fizzle.

The Bavaria was moored along the shore long before the destination was reached, and in the howling gale the Legislative Committee stepped off to the bank to escape from that angry canal.

It was decided to continue the trip by carriage! Undertaker Charles Miller provided these near Mitchell avenue.

The "raging" canal had shown it could really be a first-class rager.

It happened that about twenty years later, when another legislative committee from Columbus made another inspection of the canal on a canal excursion boat, the canal again began to show bad temper. I was with that party. The weather was wet and cold—but the delegation saw it through.

Two survivors of the famous canal ride of '89, when the Miami and Erie turned into a bucking broncho, have sent in letters about that event.

Arthur W. Davis, real estate man and former porkpacker, of 2213 Highland avenue, writes:

TERRIFIC BLIZZARD!

"Your articles are very interesting.

"Some forty years ago I was asked to contribute and to go on a jaunt on 'the raging canawl' by Fred Alms, who was always a booster for abandoning the canal. The committee from the Legislature came down; the best boat on the canal was chartered; there was a crowd, plenty to eat and drink. But it 'blew and it snew'—an awful blizzard; so we could see nothing. All were chilled to the bone, for it turned very cold and the trip was a failure; but that did not deter the backers of the improvement from working until we now have what was long hoped for—a beautiful boulevard."

OVERFLOW AND AQUEDUCT, CARTHAGE; SWIMMER ONCE WAS WASHED INTO MILLCREEK, BELOW—FRANK WILMES PHOTO.

Adam Lotz, 6254 Kincaid avenue, was also a member of the '89 excursion.

"That was a thrilling legislative junket and the canal got so wild that it 'busted' up our party," Lotz said. "A terrific wind blew, and guests and hosts nearly were frozen despite the fact that there was plenty of liquor on board as a stimulant.

PLENTY TO DRINK ON BOARD!

"We started downtown on the gaily bedecked Bavaria and it took a long time for our boat to make its way under the old Centennial Exposition buildings back of Music Hall and erected over the canal. About fifty persons were on board.

"Besides the Legislative Committee our party included Mayor Amor Smith, F. W. Alms, Henry Muhlhauser, Henry Knorr, city engineer, canal collector, Senator Richardson, President T. G. Smith of the Board of Trade, George Henshaw, Judge Pruden, Charles Muth, John Pfau, and others.

"We also had on board fine ten-year-old whisky, red wine from France, amber wine from the Rhine, cordials, sherry and plenty of other things to eat and drink.

"But all this could not keep the crowd warm when the old gale began to blow down the canal. About two miles this side of Mitchell avenue the blizzard became so wild that the canal trip, though unfinished, had to be given up. The rest of the route was covered in carriages.

"The placid canal had won its first victory against those who wanted to transform it into a boulevard."

From Nick Altrock

Nick Altrock, a Cincinnati product, who was raised on the canal, became a famous pitcher and, later, comedian of baseball, writes from Washington, D. C.:

"I jumped into the canal once—to get away from Dad's big stick!" and he humbly signs himself:

"NICK ALTROCK,
"The funniest man in baseball."

Congressman Tatgenhorst Graduate of Towpath, Too!

Congressman Charles Tatgenhorst writes as follows: As a boy I often swam in the old canal near the place depicted in the recent issue of the Times-Star. As usual, it was against the wishes of my parents, who realized I could not swim. Many paddlings did I receive for doing this, but nevertheless kept on and on one occasion was almost drowned. In passing the old place it brings back to me many fond and pleasant memories. Not having bathing suits, we usually hid in the bushes when the canal boats came. On occasions we found our clothes tied in knots.

Boat Ride to Toledo

Fifty years ago I took a trip with Capt. Minster, on boat Niagara, to Toledo, O. Both captain and I had fishing tackle and shotguns, and when we struck a good place to hunt or fish we would stay a day or so, and, believe me, that was the happy time of my life—in my 'teens.—Henry Pell, 1273 Parkway, Covington, Ky.

Boys Built Their Boat Too Large for Door!

Four of us boys built a flatboat to use on the canal, in the cellar on Elm street where one of the boys lived. We worked on the boat for several days and nights. We finished it nicely and calked all tightly.

You should have seen our chagrin when we picked it up and found we had made it so large we could not get it out of the cellar. Well, we had to take it apart and put it together again on the sidewalk. The four of us carried it triumphantly and launched it in the canal. We climbed in, but the boat leaked so that it soon sank and we had to swim to shore.—Alfred W. Macbrair, College Hill.

HULL OF OLD BOAT IN CANAL OPPOSITE CLIFTON SPRINGS DISTILLERY—PHOTO BY W. H. BOONE.

"The Canal Gave Me a Thousand Happy Memories," Says Fries

"I can easily qualify for membership in the Canal Swimmers' Society, for I engaged in every sport on the canal," said George Fries, assistant general manager of the Times-Star.

"People like to recall those good old days when life was not so rushed and hurried. The canal-boat era was slow, but it had its compensations. In general it was a kindly, more restful age, neighborly and tranquil.

"I was born on Central avenue, near Dayton street, close to the canal, and the old towpath was my playground. I swam, skated, boated, jumped on the canal boats and saw the cutting of the ice and the loading of the ice and sand boats. The canal has given me a thousand happy memories and a great many stirring ones, too. I was a very small boy when I saw the great fire that destroyed the old Procter & Gamble soap factory on the canal bank. And a deep fright came over all us boys when an older boy on Halloween night playfully pursued another lad along the canal bank and struck him on the head with a 'sausage,' or stuffed stocking, badly injuring him.

"If the pursued boy had been bold enough to jump into the canal he would have escaped."

"Stream of Happiness," Says Rev. Baum of Canal

Being one of the boys who spent much of their playtime on the canal towpath, I think I am eligible to join the Canal Society. The old stream exerted a wonderful attraction upon us. Our favorite meeting place was the aqueduct over the Millcreek at Carthage. From the top of the aqueduct we made our heroic leaps and neck-breaking dives into its waters. In the winter we would skate and enjoy hard-fought games of "shinny."

We also spent much time on the towpath watching the loading of canal boats at the docks of gravel pits, and then get a ride on the sand carts to the barn. We knew most of the boats by name. One of the very interesting happenings on the canal was the annual visit of the old mud digger, which we would watch for hours.

We are happy that there has been builded the new and beautiful parkway, but let us not forget that the old canal was a stream of happiness for many of the boys who today are the prosperous business men of the Queen City of the West.—The Rev. Emil E. Baum, Riverside Drive, city.

Found $20 on Water, But Also Received Whipping

Well do I remember, it was back in the '60s, my father had forbidden me to go swimming, but the temptation was too great and I would go in anyway. One day to my great surprise I found a $20 bill floating on the water. I took it home immediately to my father and told him how I had found it on top of the water while swimming. He took the twenty, gave me a quarter and a whipping besides for disobeying him, but never after that did I ever have him forbid swimming in the canal.—William Felix, Westwood.

Nice Trick! Put Paper On Holes in Ice!

I was saved from drowning when playing shinny on the ice at Main street bridge. The boys cut holes in the ice and covered them up with newspapers. Great trick! I tried to walk across the canal on a pair of stilts and got stuck in the mud.—George F. Brossart, 4437 Plainville road.

BOYS ON CLIFTON AVENUE BRIDGE OVER CANAL WATCH STEAM SHOVEL—PHOTO BY W. H. BOONE.

Alfred S. Wood, 90, Joins Club; Grandfather Started Canal Work, 1825

Alfred S. Wood, aged 90, who played on the canal bank and fell into its waters eighty-six years ago, and whose grandfather, John O. Clark, had the honor of wheeling the first wheelbarrow of dirt when the canal work was started at Cincinnati in 1825, has just joined the Canal Swimmers' Society.

Wood, born in Cincinnati in 1838, lives at 443 Dayton street, and writes:

I resided on West Eighth street for twenty-one years, corner of Baldwin alley, that ran north to the canal. On the north side, east of Race street, stood the "Ballance" sheepskin tannery, from which a small stream flowed into the canal and was one of my choice fishing places for sunfish for many of my boy days. I did my share of "shinny" and skating on the canal from Vine street to Mohawk.

When a child of four years I fell into the canal, and was pushed in many times afterward. My grandfather, John O. Clark, came to this city in 1819, and when they started to dig the canal in this city in 1825 he wheeled the first wheelbarrow of dirt out onto the bank. At that time it was a great honor.

"Cops" in White Dusters!

"In 1862, when I swam in the canal, the police wore white dusters with a star badge in the summer time, and carried a cane," said Anthony Corry, 2603 Dennis street. "One day the police chased us and we ran, naked, into the Findlay Market, and dressed. We had the clothes of a boy named Adolph Smith, and the policeman covered Adolph with his duster and took him to the station house. Years later Adolph became police lieutenant."

Canal Romance! Skated, And Then, Were Married!

My particular event which remains a pleasant memory was just forty-two years ago.

I became acquainted with a charming miss from South avenue and she wanted to learn to skate. I said, "Let's go to the canal." We enjoyed the skating fine.

We were married by the Rev. L. W. Joyce of St. Paul M. E. Church April 15, 1886, and no sign of divorce yet.—J. L. Davis, 1516 North Bend road.

Practical Joker Floated, Looking Like Corpse!

John Koch, 67 De Camp avenue, noted local pitcher and acrobat in his youth, writes that he learned his acrobatic stunts on the sand on the banks of the canal. John, who was better known as Manny, tells of a prank he used to play. He would get into the canal with all his clothes on and float down the middle of the stream, like a corpse. People passing by would raise a cry of alarm and call the police—and then Manny would swim to the other side and laughingly "run for his life."

Always Remember It As "The Towpath"

I have today received from my sister, Mrs. Harry Whiting Brown of Glendale, O., a copy of the Times-Star containing pictures and description of portions of the dear old canal, and the beautiful new boulevard. I hope it may always be known and referred to as "The Towpath." I imagine every man who ever knew it and played on or around the canal would prefer that name. From 1865 until 1869 I played on the canal.— M. B. McIntyre, 154 Eighth avenue, Brooklyn, N. Y.

Brighton House, Capitol of "Porkopolis," Was Often Scene of Jolly Revelries!

FAMED BRIGHTON HOUSE—PICTURE LOANED BY C. F. HUSS.

Three quarters of a century ago the Brighton House, located on the right bank of the canal at Brighton, was one of the busiest places in Cincinnati, then famous as "Porkopolis."

Farmers, hog raisers, drovers, herders and hog dealers from all parts of the country came to Brighton, national center of the packing industry. This created an urgent demand for a hotel. On the site of the old Zenith Inn the imposing five-story Brighton House was built, with its great verandas overlooking the canal scene. On the tower was a bull—the symbol of the glory that was then Brighton's. The old hostelry has long since been torn down.

"In the course of time gaming became general in the house," says an account in "Historic Brighton." "Poker and other games were in full blast nightly in all parts of the house and the attractions of so general and varied a nature drew men of all classes until finally the neighborhood was invested with objectionable characters.

"The conditions grew worse until about 1859, when citizens of the neighborhood became aroused to action and decided to take matters in their own hands. A vigilance committee was formed and it started a war on recklessness. The offenders were put to rout, peace and order were restored and Brighton started on a new era."

Mother's Ring Lost

I remember the first time I went swimming in the old and dearly beloved canal; that is, I tried to swim but could not. It was a long time before I could swim—it was back in 1874. Well, I lost my mother's gold ring and of course I expected to receive a grand lecture, but I came through without a reprimand.—Joseph McClellan, 1803 Chase street.

Boat Named "Friend"

I recall canal boat rides on the Elizabeth, Australia and Friend.

We rode from here to Toledo and I saw the boys swimming, the driver falling off the mules and the boat dragging him along, also the boys hanging on the boat as we went along the canal. I was twelve then. Now I am seventy-eight.—Mrs. Lizzie Dorsch, 1647 Freeman avenue.

> **Thousands Dove In! One Obeyed Mother!
> He Stayed Ashore! John Rettig—No Other!**

Can this society admit a "good" boy?

> How good was he?
>
> He stood on the canal bank over fifty years ago and "saw a thousand boys, undressed and lined up on the shore ready to plunge into the then clear and refreshing stream."
>
> At the stroke of 8 p. m. from a factory bell on the canal bank he saw these thousand boys leap and dive and plunge joyously into the canal for their nightly swim—
>
> But our applicant for membership was so good that he alone, of the entire thousand, remained on the shore, high and dry.

How he longed to join his playmates in the water, dashing, splashing, crashing merrily in the canal!

But his mother told him not to go in—and he was such a good boy that he resisted the temptation and stayed out—the only one of a thousand!

Who was this remarkable martyr in the cause of filial obedience?

> **None other than John Rettig, our own beloved Cincinnati artist.**

This presents an entirely new problem for the Membership Committee of the club—no other applicant could have resisted the temptation to dive in.

He tells about his experience in a letter.

"My dear Ludwig," he writes, "can I get into the Canal Swimmers' Society?

"Well do I remember the canal bank—Findlay to Bank street was a favorite swimming hole of the boys.

"At 7 the boys began to arrive—the canal reflected the evening sky like a mirror. At 7:30 it began to darken and the boys began to undress with much noise, and sat along the bank.

> "Suddenly, when the Procter & Gamble factory bell struck 8, a thousand boys at the same moment dived into the canal. The spray splashed high and the water was a cauldron of animation and youthful pandemonium as far as eye could see.

"Duckings were in order.

"Bad boys, during the swim, left the water and tied fast knots in the uninitiated boys' trouser legs and shirt sleeves called 'green apples.'

"I was not allowed to go in the canal and must have been an obedient boy, receiving a ticket for the Schmidt Bath House in the river.

"But I was at the Findlay street bridge every night.

"They say my brother Martin was carried on older boys' backs across the canal before he could walk. Mister, can I belong to the Canal Swimmers' Society?—Cordially, John Rettig."

We have so many "bad" boys, members of old-time fighting street gangs, and cop-teasers, in our society, that we really need one good boy who obeyed mother.

Mr. Rettig not only played, but worked, on the banks of the canal, and made sketches along its waters. In 1878, when a student at the Art

CANAL VISTA UP PLUM STREET—WILMES PHOTO.

Academy, he painted the organ pipes in Music Hall. In '81 he began the painting of scenes for operatic and dramatic productions in Music Hall and continued this for many years. For the Centennial Exposition of 1888, he created the notable spectacle, "The Egyptian Cinderella," and the canal pageant, "The Carnival of Venice."

Mr. Rettig has spent years painting canals in Holland and in Venice—just returned from the latter city, where he made sixty-six canal paintings!

President of Reds Is Canal Swimmer, Too!

"Yes, I'm a canal swimmer, too," said J. C. McDiarmid, president of the Cincinnati Baseball Club Company, "and it is a pleasure to recall those happy boyhood days. We lived in the West End in the early '80s and I often swam in the canal, played on the banks and took part with our crowd in some memorable engagements with the boys on Fairview Heights."

Swimming Hole, Pear Orchard Made a Great Combination!

"The White Fence was the best place to swim along the canal," says J. B. Wetterer, "for there were no houses on either side, and no fear of being frightened by the cry of 'The Cop!'

"It was where the Vogel packing house is located, 2604 Colerain avenue. There used to be a fine pear orchard at the place and a high, whitewashed fence."

Picture of Canal Bridge Barricade Recalls Courthouse Riot of '84 When Many Lost Lives

The most exciting and terrifying scenes ever witnessed along the placid old canal were during the Courthouse riots of 1884.

The picture on the opposite page, from the Cincinnati Gazette of April 2, 1884, was loaned by Emil Wendel, 14 East McMillan street, and shows the barricade across the canal bridge at Main street, just above the Courthouse.

The riot followed public resentment at the failure of the courts and juries to mete out "adequate justice" in a series of murder cases. Twenty-three prisoners accused of murder or homicide were in the jail before the riots. Following the case in Avondale in which two body snatchers were accused of murdering a family to secure their bodies for the dissecting table came the climax in the William Berner case. Berner and Joseph Palmer, the latter a mulatto, had beaten the life out of their employer, William Kirk, for a small sum of money, so Historian Greve relates. Berner, defended by T. C. Campbell, was found by the jury to be guilty only of manslaughter. Judge Samuel R. Matthews "was aroused into an indignant denunciation of this miscarriage of justice," and on March 28 imposed the full limit of the law, twenty years in the penitentiary. That night a crowd of 8,000 took part in a protest meeting in Music Hall, addressed by such prominent citizens as Dr. Andrew C. Kemper, Judge A. G. W. Carter and Gen. Andrew Hickenlooper. They contemplated no riot—but after the meeting the cry was raised: "To the jail!"—and to the jail the great crowd surged. Morton L. Hawkins, then sheriff, is still living. The mob battered down the jail doors with heavy timbers—but Berner had been started to Columbus. Police, fire department and militia were called out. The Courthouse was burned, and it is estimated that over fifty people were killed and several hundred wounded in the rioting that lasted several days.

Treasure in Pied Type Buried in Canal Bed!

As John C. Hillen, printer, "makeup" man on this book, put the type in orderly rotation, he recalled his first experience with "canal type." His parents lived near the canal and he was a canal swimmer. One day, while carrying several galleys of type across the Sycamore street bridge—Hillen was then a young printer's apprentice—a bunch of Woodward high school students, racing across the bridge, accidentally bumped into him and sent his type flying into the middle of the canal. And there it lies today, a sort of sunken treasure, all pied, deep in the old canal bed under the boulevard!

Fish and Snake Yarn!

I caught a five-inch fish in the canal. Left it on the hook and next morning found a snake on my line. It had swallowed the fish. I killed the snake. It was six feet long!—Henry Alexander, 253 Helen street.

Canal Tragedy! Mud Ball Sank Brand New Sunday Hat!

"Despite mother's admonitions, the canal was the playground of my youth," said Joseph F. Illig, foreman of the job printing department of the Times-Star and printer of this canal book. "I swam in it, dove, jumped on the canal boats, was shoved off the embankment and fell in through the sink holes in the ice. But the greatest tragedy—the wind blew my brand new confirmation hat into the canal. We threw mud in to make waves and wash the hat ashore, but it filled and sank out of sight forever as the last piece of mud fell into the hat instead of just beyond it!"

Slow Old Days Had Beauty and Happiness!

I am thankful for the beautiful Central Parkway, but I can not help saying that in those old slow canal days there were beauty and happiness. Everyone lived to let live.—E. J. Berry, 2509 Chatham street.

MAIN STREET CANAL BRIDGE BARRICADE IN COURTHOUSE RIOT OF 1884—LOANED BY EMIL WENDEL.

> **This Lad Played Every Towpath Game—
> 'Twas B. H. Kroger of Business Fame!**

The canal, in the old days, appealed as a playground alike to high and low, rich and poor.

And today all alike enjoy the pleasant reminiscences of the good old days along the towpath.

B. H. Kroger, in youth an ardent canal swimmer, skater and navigator, became one of the great business leaders of the city, bank president and founder of the Kroger Grocery and Baking Company. He was a member, too, of the Rapid Transit Commission.

And he has never forgotten those carefree days along the old towpath.

From his winter home in Florida he writes that he had the happiest times of his life on the canal—and would like to live them over again.

Dear Ludwig:

I think the happiest times of my life were spent as a boy along the canal.

I was born on what was known as Western Row, now Central avenue, just above Fourteenth street. On the corner of Fourteenth and Plum was the old Spence Pork House and north of that Sanning's Planing Mill, where they had an old steer supplying the power for the mill. An old man who lived next to the mill had a boat on the canal and many times we were booted off his boat. But one Saturday morning three of us got in the boat and he left us stay in—in fact, we could not get off until we reached St. Bernard. There he left us off to walk home and get what was coming to us—and without any dinner. We did not arrive home until six o'clock that evening, a tired and hungry trio.

It was our habit when going home from school to have one of the boys carry the clothes while the rest of the boys jumped in the canal at Clay street and swam to Fourteenth street. One day it was my turn to carry the clothes, while among the boys swimming there was a "big bully." This gave us a good chance to even up matters with him. So every time he attempted to get out of the water we threw sand on him and back into the canal he had to go to clean himself. We kept him in the water until two o'clock. School began at one. Result: No lunch, a beating at school, two black eyes afterwards and a paddling at home.

The canal was the great rendezvous of the Texas gang, on the west side, and Mohawks, on the east. At Fourteenth and the canal was a free-stone works where old workmen would split huge stones with a crowbar. The boys liked to use the splinters of these stones as missiles and on my knee I still carry a big scar made by one of the Mohawks.

Many times have I gone through the ice while skating in winter and many times in summer have I stood on a board and paddled it on the canal from Fourteenth street to the elbow.

Even now I wish for the good old days of boyhood. With best wishes for your health and happiness,

Yours,   B. H. KROGER.

BEAUTIFUL MUMMERT'S BASIN SWIMMING HOLE, CLIFTON, BEYOND SECOND BASIN—PHOTO BY W. H. BOONE.

The Girls Enjoyed the Towpath, Too!
So Here's a "Woman's Page" for You!

Look Out! A Water Snake!

One day when sitting on the bank, fishing for a beautiful fan just out of reach, I fell in. For a while I floundered about, but, seeing a large water snake, I began using my arms and legs as the boys did, and swam to the shore before a man, who was coming to get me out, arrived. Now isn't that enough swimming to make me eligible to the Canal Swimmers' Society?—Mrs. William H. Lonney, 2618 Hemlock street.

Mother Put Dresses On This Canal Boy!

I remember a boy lived next door to us on Vine, near Twelfth street, whose mother used to put dresses on him so he would not go in swimming! Those were happy old days. I wish I had them back again.—Mrs. Albert Mueller, 1424 Republic street.

"It Was Beautiful!"

A crowd of us used to go skiff riding on the canal. My brother played the mouth harp and we took our mandolin and guitar with us, and played and sang. We generally went on moonlight nights, and it was beautiful. We had a glorious time.—Mrs. Bettie Mitchell, 3824 Odin avenue, Kennedy Heights.

Ah! The Volga! And Dancing on the Bridge!

It surely was wonderful to us, in the good old canal days, to ride along and have music and singing all the way and then wind up dancing on the canal bridge. The Volga boatmen had nothing on us.—Mrs. William Switzer, 4316 Williams place, Northside.

Another Romance! Plighted Troth on Canal Bridge!

When I was a schoolgirl I went rowing with some companions, fell into the water, and was romantically rescued by a devoted young man.

Years later, my fiance, a Cincinnati boy, and I, with sufficiently picturesque surroundings, stood on the Hopple street bridge and arranged our wedding ceremony. The nuptial knot has remained intact ever since (though tied many years ago).—Mr. and Mrs. A. L. Fillmore, Pittsburgh, Pa.

Rode on Sleigh When Canal Was Frozen Over

When the ice was thick we rode with a sleigh and a horse on the canal from east of Glendale to Lockland, where they were cutting ice. The ride and skating were wonderful. And why shouldn't I belong to the Canal Swimmers' Society when my father, H. H. Lippelman, at one time owned and operated a fleet of eleven canal boats, and my brothers and my son swam in the canal?—Mrs. Anne Lippelman Anderson, Greenwood avenue, Glendale, O.

Sunday School Picnic! And Baskets Filled With Goodies!

I can recall our Sunday picnics on the canal, as a child, and the pleasure we had riding to Ludlow Grove. Mother would fill a basket with goodies, and we thought we were great to ride a canal boat drawn by two mules, and we would sing our Sunday School hymns. The boat was like a large barge, and our seats were only plain boards laid from one side to the other, but to us old-timers this was a real treat.—Mrs. Louise Graf Piott, 422 West McMicken avenue.

> See the Lovely Ladies, on the Towpath Shore!
> Only Toe-Tips Visible—Nary One Inch More!

HATS LARGER, DRESSES LONGER IN CANAL DAYS!

C. W. Boebinger, teacher of drawing and industrial design, Ohio Mechanics' Institute, loaned this charming canal picture. It shows the Camera Club of the institute on an outing along the canal some years ago, when large hats and long dresses were the vogue, and only ankles showed. The picture was snapped at the Ludlow avenue bridge, Mt. Storm Park entrance, and named on the photo are Hilda Knost, Julia Clark, Alice Hetzel, Lottie Tucker, Louise Becker and Amy Sage. One of the girls snapped the picture.

Horse Jumped In!

Years ago Kahn, the Vine street clothier, who called himself "Kahn, the Misfit Man," drove up Vine in his buggy. The horse took fright, broke from the harness and leaped right into the canal. We had a jolly time getting the horse out.—L. P. Ezekiel.

How One Crowd Made Their Sandy Beach!

One time a sand boat got stuck in the canal at Rush street. All of us children got shovels, and how we shoveled sand into our swimming spot!—Mrs. Thomas Lynch, Dayton, Ky.

Found Cannon Ball in '65! Great Was His Joy! Dropped It in Canal! Lost His Precious Toy!

H. P. Smith, president of the People's Banking Company, Lewisburg, O., tells an interesting story of how he found a cannon ball during the Civil War and lost this unusual toy in the canal, where his crowd searched in vain for it for a year.

"The first time that I took a swim in the canal was in 1856, during the Fremont campaign," he writes.

My saddest experience was during the Civil War. There was a foundry at Liberty and Canal, in which they made munitions. They used to test out their guns west of Clifton avenue, on what is now Wheeler street. There were no houses up there, excepting a small frame building at the head of Elm street. Our boys used to go up and watch from a distance. One day after they were through I found a six-pound cannon ball, and I felt happy. I took the ball down to the canal to show to the other boys, and while there concluded to take a swim. One of the boys suggested we take the ball, toss it in the air, let it drop in the water, then dive down after it. We did that once too often. The cannon ball went down in the soft mud and we could not find it, and for a year at least every time we went to swim we would dive down and try to find it. But it was gone, and I often wondered, when they built the subway, if they found it. It was lost back of the old Procter & Gamble factory, about ten feet from the towpath."

Boat and Bridge Jumper

A few of my canal experiences: Jumping in canal after iceboat unloaded from Stone Lake in the rear of Stone Lake Ice Company on Central avenue. Jumping off the bridge and diving. Jumping on steering rudder of canal boat Nanna Laurel, shown in the Times-Star. I swam in the canal alongside of dead dogs, chickens and hogs and am today in perfect health!—William Eisenecher, 1669 Montrose street.

Mule Pulled Skiff

J. R. Pigman, 6119 Tulane road, Pleasant Ridge: We had a wonderful skiff ride on the canal years ago. A canal boat driver came along with a lone mule and kindly hitched our skiff to his rope. The mule pulled us along the canal at a stiff pace, and I had my leg out in the water and got a ducking.

Well! Lady Godiva! Chased by a "Cop"

I dove from the old Sycamore street bridge in broad daylight and, dressed in the costume of Lady Godiva, was chased by a cop for three blocks. I spent hours in untying the "green apples" that I found in my clothing.—George A. J. Gampfer, 223 East Third street.

Great Bonfires On Canal At Elections

Well do I remember the election bonfires along the canal. Each gang trying to outdo the other with the most barrels blazing high on top of each other. We would gather ash barrels and boxes for two weeks before election and hide them for the final night.—Leo Albert, 1573 Pullan avenue.

FISHING IN ROSS LAKE, LONG POPULAR FOR BOATING, SWIMMING, ANGLING—PHOTO BY C. W. FEHRMANN.

Backward, Turn Backward, O Time in Your Flight, Make Me a Child Again, Just For Tonight!

The covered aqueduct over the canal, near Carthage, pictured on another page, was a favorite swimming pool of the Hartwell boys, writes James R. Duncan, Jr., Burton Apartments, Covington. There were cross-rods and timbers fifteen to eighteen feet above the water in the aqueduct roof and the agile boys would climb to these timbers and dive down into the canal below.

Sometimes they would use the rods for doing their acrobatic and trapeze stunts.

"The first time I climbed up to a lofty perch on that roof over the water to dive off, I lost my balance and fell off, instead," Duncan relates. "We used to play 'catchers,' and the boy who was 'it' pursued the rest and they leaped like frogs off the roof timbers, or climbed across, hand over hand. Kerplunk, one would dive into the water far below, and the pursuer would follow suit. Ah, if time would turn backward and make us boys again, for a day!"

Horseshoe Luck! Clothes Stolen! Wore Sack Home!

I dived in near the old Fifteenth street bridge. Placed my cap and clothes on a tuft of grass near a sand pile, and a horseshoe on top to keep the wind from blowing them away. When I got out on the bank, I discovered that someone had taken my wardrobe, but a farmer's wife, loading potatoes in a cart from a boat nearby, came to my rescue with a potato sack. She cut two holes in the bottom to slip my feet through, pulled it up as far as she could, cut two slits for my arms, and tied the top of the sack around my neck, and said, "Now run home, little boy, as fast as you can"—and I did.—Letter from the David Davis School, 2519 May street.

At 80 Still Would Like To Swim in Canal!

I remember as a small boy going from Cincinnati to Piqua, O., on a canal passenger packet. Later, a crowd of us skated to Lockland. The canal was frozen over beautifully. We found the ice-breaker ready to break up the ice, but the boat caught fire and burned.

My eightieth birthday has not dimmed my memory of skating on, falling into, and swimming in the canal. I would like to take a swim in the old place today. As it is, I have to do my swimming during the winter in Florida.—W. T. Mitchell, 200 Provident Bank.

Florida Heard From!

I have not resided in Cincinnati for forty-two years. In the good old days from 1865 to 1870 I often played on the canal. What fun it used to be to wade in the canal mud and catch crawfish when the water happened to be temporarily out of the canal.—J. O. Wright, Green Cove Springs, Fla.

"Feather-Edged" Rowing

Your account would not be complete if it did not mention the Clipsetta Boat Club, that operated the Grace Darling and the Ivy Leaf, the rowers of which were John Falls and Ed Falls, and Joseph and Michael Wopperrer. Their "feather-edged" rowing in the early nineties were the admiration of the "canal bank" inhabitants, and their modern songs in harmony, such as "Two Little Girls in Blue," "Just Break the News to Mother," etc., were beauteous and made the whole canal neighborhood sit up and listen.—A Canal Swimmer.

Hot Swimming Race!

My most thrilling experience was the time I won a swimming contest from A. E. Lippelman, starting at the "Old Elm Tree," upstream to "Kemper's Bridge," a distance of thirteen telegraph poles. Along the towpath, in close pursuit, riding two mules, came the judges of the contest—C. W. Hoffman (now a real judge) and W. G. Lippelman. I won by a neck, but they gave me a bum deal when they declared it a dead heat.—Roger Meagher, Glendale.

AH, THE FUN OF PLAYING ON OLD SUNKEN CANAL BOAT HULLS IN THE SUBURBS!—W. H. BOONE PHOTO.

Magnificent, Towered "Castles on the Rhine" Made Canal View at Clifton Wondrous Fine!

Entrancingly beautiful was the view presented to the canal traveler as he reached Clifton. There, on the top of the green-clad hill, he beheld three magnificent castles, with their graceful towers, in a setting of ivy and trees, and the scenes of many famous social functions.

These were the noted Probasco, Schoenberger and Bowler residences. The grounds of the latter, opening on Ludlow avenue at the canal, were bought by Mr. Bowler in 1846, and fortunately are now owned by the city as a park. Years ago the Prince of Wales danced in the lovely Bowler mansion on the hilltop, a fine two-story building surmounted by a square tower, and with pillars across the front porch. In the garden is a Greek summer house, copy of the famous Temple of Love in the Petite Trianon Palace in France.

The Probasco mansion was built during the Civil War and was gorgeously decorated with heavily carved mahogany and walnut and other adornments in black and white marble, crystal and ebony.

The Schoenberger mansion was built in the sixties and was distinguished for its magnificent carvings in oak, its picture gallery with its famous paintings, the dining room with its oaken sideboard and grinning masks of Bacchus carved on the doors of the wine closets and grand staircase with its carved owl, kept company by a line of bats up the stairs. Later the fine residence was acquired as the "Scarlet Oaks" Hospital.

The lovely Probasco residence, Oakwood, later the Reakirt home, was decorated with a wealth of carving paying tribute to the oak—iron gates with oak-leaf design, massive stone posts carved in oak leaves and acorns, heavy interior woodwork in golden oak carrying further the oak suggestion. The carving was done by Ben Pitman and he spent three years on the grand staircase alone.

He Was Thrown In!

One of the older boys threw me in and gently instructed me to take my choice between swimming and drowning. The result was that I swam across the canal seven times. After that I did not need to be thrown in.—Warren W. Porter, Mt. Healthy.

Driver Fell Dead!

Years ago I saw a man who was driving a mule, drawing a canal boat, fall off the mule because of an attack of heart disease. He fell into the water, and was dead.—W. A. Mintern, 629 Washington avenue, Newport.

Says: "Beautify Millcreek By Use of Canal Flow!"

Horace Johnson, Lockland, employe of the State in the canal service, declares that during dry spells the water of the canal, which flows into Millcreek, keeps Millcreek from becoming stagnant.

"The canal water is today the cleanest water in the Millcreek Valley and keeps Millcreek flowing," he said. He urges that Millcreek be cleaned up through the construction of trunk sewers and that the canal water, flowing through Millcreek, will make it possible to create a beautiful waterway once more out of Millcreek.

Limburger! Pretzels! Pigs' Feet! So John Had a Good Time!

I was a member of Race Street Willing Workers. Used to meet Saturday nights back of Knox's ice house, chip in, get a keg of beer, big limburger, sour pigs' feet, sack of fresh pretzels. Music, swimming and good time, and never cost us over 25 cents each. Those were the good old days. Hauck's beer! Right from the cellars.— John Theobald, 2343 Victor street.

ENTRANCING CANAL VIEW, BACK OF CLIFTON—PHOTO BY FRANK WILMES.

Frank Wilmes, Cincinnati Artist, Holds Record As Star Diver

Frank Wilmes, the artist, who has a fine collection of old canal pictures, some of which are printed in this book, through his kindness, is an honorary member of the Canal Society, and is awarded the title of Champion Canal Diver.

Sixty years ago, when scarcely ten, he swam in the canal at Camp Washington. He caught catfish, skated, swam and rode on the canal boats. His favorite stunt was to stand on one shore, dive into the water and come up, touching the opposite bank. He was the only lad in the crowd that could do this.

"Well do I remember the old passenger boats on the canal of some sixty years ago," Wilmes said. "They traveled from Cincinnati to Toledo and were decorated with bunting and flags. They had sleeping rooms, along two-thirds of the length of the boat, and the windows had pretty curtains."

Faithful, in Ascension Robes, Gathered On Brighton Hill in 1843, Expecting End of World!

In June, 1843, passengers on the canal, looking up Brighton Hill, saw a strange sight. The religious sect of Millerites, believing the end of the world was near and that they were about to ascend to Heaven, gathered on Brighton Hill, where a platform was erected.

"A vast concourse assembled there at daylight on the morning of the eventful day, dressed in their ascension robes," it is recorded in the book, "Historic Brighton." "The entire day was spent in calm and patient waiting for developments—but there were none. The would-be ascensionists continued to inhabit the earth. Sadly disappinted, they returned to their homes and took up the daily tasks they had forsaken. Little was heard of the Millerites after this."

Brighton, with its many packing houses, its distilleries, tanneries and other factories, was one of the busiest ports along the canal seventy-five years ago.

Brighton claims to have given Cincinnati its name and fame as "Porkopolis" in those days. When one of the packers there slaughtered 2,000 hogs in a day, the news went all over the country. Fleets of canal boats would be moored at Brighton, delivering raw and manufactured supplies—whisky, hogs, cattle, corn, cord wood.

Lead pipes carried water from the canal to various parts of Brighton in the early days—mostly for watering animals. At the Gibbons tannery a wolf and a dog were harnessed to a treadmill that pumped the tannery's water supply.

In 1840 Samuel J. Browne's large estate, homestead and orchard adjoined the canal, extending from Browne street, now McMicken avenue, to the top of Brighton Hill. Long ago Daniel Gano raised a grove of mulberry trees in this district, for propagating silk worms. But the silk industry did not succeed and the grove was later called "Buffalo Patch," for Gano kept a small herd of buffalo there.

Michael Haag, who conducted a summer garden at Brighton, constructed a drawbridge of rafts over the canal, and for a charge of five cents per person it gave passage to the pretty woods and picnic grounds on the other side. Haag also built the circular building known as the Round House opposite the bridge, converting the grounds into a summer garden where concerts were given.

"It was erroneously believed that the famous Mrs. Frances Trollope lived in the Round House—but she came to Cincinnati in 1826, and the Round House was not built until about Civil War times, for I remember as a boy watching its construction," said Jacob Hoffmann, Brighton historian. The house is shown on next page.

The boys of the Brighton and nearby Mohawk district often tried to conquer each other—but they made common cause when the "Texans," from farther down, tried to invade their canal territory.

Joe's "Big Fish" Story

Forty years ago the Lotus Club used to take the canal boat up to Knorr's ice house at Lesourdsville, camp on the banks of the canal, adjoining the ice house, and fish in Knorr's pond, covering twenty-two acres. The sunfish were so plentiful that I often caught two of them on the hook at one time. One day a large fish, measuring about eighteen inches in length, jumped into our boat, and in our efforts to hold the fish down, we almost capsized the boat.—Joseph D. Engelbert.

Hot Toddies! Here's Official Bartender!

Louis Webb—I had many playdays along the canal, but especially do I remember the day that I fell through the ice while skating—because that experience got me two nice, hot toddies, to warm my frozen body. It was grand medicine, worth falling into the canal for. Sometimes the ice would move in undulating waves as we skated on it and we called that "rubber ice."

THE CANAL AT BRIGHTON, WITH PICTURESQUE OLD "ROUND HOUSE"—PHOTO BY ELMER L. FOOTE.

> "Canal Life Was Grand!" Said Grizzled Sea Dog;
> Always Plenty Water—at Times a Bit o' Grog!"

> Beautiful canal through lovely woodlands. . . .
> Whiskey, five cents a tin cup full!
> Prettiest mules—big fellows—friendly as a child—
> Mule driver at 13—pilot, captain—
> Women unloading wheel hubs from boat!
> Caught seventy-pound catfish! Wild foxes!
> Caught opossum and raccoon. . . .
> Flying squirrels in trees!
> My wife cooking in the canal boat cabin. . . .

These memories flitted through the mind of Capt. Ben Hoffman, oldest surviving Cincinnati canal boat captain, as he told of his career as mule driver, pilot and captain on the canal starting sixty-three years ago, when he was but 13. The grizzled old sea dog laughed as he said:

"I'm 76—but I used to like 'Old 76' in former days!"

The captain never knocked a Canal Swimmer off his boat and NEVER KICKED A MULE!

On occasion our captain liked his grog—but he LOVED HIS MULES.

"Oh, I had the prettiest mules!" he exclaimed, "great big fellows, and as gentle as a child. They were easy-going, hard-working animals. I never had a bit of trouble with 'em.

"I never whipped one in my life—and the one thing I wouldn't stand for was for one of my drivers to beat a mule.

"There were five bunks in the forward cabin for the canal drivers and crew, bunks in the stern cabin, where the kitchen was, for the captain and his wife, and pilot—and the mules slept in stalls between. There were also two big rooms amidship for freight. I always got credit for having the finest mules, free of shoulder sores.

"For years I made the run from Cincinnati to Hamilton.

"Sometimes we would stop at Crescentville or Port Union for a drink of beer. I often carried cargoes of beer and whiskey. When we loaded whiskey the distillery gave us four gallons for the men who did the unloading—and of course I helped, too.

"Made many trips to Dayton—and once made a canal boat trip all the way to Toledo, crossed the lake in a tug and got lake ice and brought it to Cincinnati.

"Saw many snapping turtles in the canal and caught many. In the early days the flying squirrels could be seen flying from tree to tree on the shore and we often saw rabbits and other small game.

"I caught a baby opossum and raccoon and made pets out of them—had them on the boat and carried one in each hand when I got off the boat.

"I worked the canal boats 'Silvery Moon,' 'Florida, 'Lock City,' and many others. B. M. Kennedy, Lawrence Larsh, Hamilton; William McKinney and H. H. Lippelman were early boat owners.

Ah! Pretty Willow Patch

"John Clark of Cincinnati and Capt. Hancey of Sycamore street are old surviving captains—but so far as I know I am the oldest here. Our

CAPT. BEN HOFFMAN—HE NEVER BEAT HIS MULES.

crew would consist of two mule drivers, a bowsman, to watch the front, and two pilots. The pilots each served a trick going to Hamilton. We changed tricks at Willow Patch, two miles above Lockland."

At Willow Patch! What a lovely name! What a beautiful place it must have been—or still is.

Capt. Hoffman served on the canal gasoline boats Ajax and Monitor. He served on the electric mule, too—but that went against his grain.

"I loved my regular mules—but I had no use for those darned old electric mules—nothing but a flat car with a motor to pull the boats with a 170-foot steel cable. Work on them was like switching cars in a railroad yard," the old captain said with contempt.

"When we had real mules we could ride till we got tired and then get off and walk till we got tired. That was the life! And you could talk to those mules. They were good company.

"Often carried a cargo of a hundred kegs of beer. We did not go dry on board. I have taken many Sunday picnickers to Woodsdale Island.

"One day my pal and I sampled those five-cent level cupful drinks to be had at Court and Walnut streets and I fell in the canal. He tried to help me out—and I pulled him in! Oh, it was lots of fun.

"But I have not taken a drink since prohibition."

"Electric Mule" Built To Replace Living Mule, But Soon Passed Out of Existence

The "electric mule" tracks, seen in the picture on the opposite page, were laid along the canal bank more than twenty-five years ago. The picture was loaned by the Union Gas and Electric Company, whose president, H. C. Blackwell, president also of the Chamber of Commerce, joined the Canal Club, for he went to school on the canal bank in the old Technical School in Music Hall.

"The idea of the 'electric mule' was to have an electric motor truck, running on rails, pull the canal boats, and thus abolish the use of living mules," said Felix J. Koch, who took a ride on the electric mules in 1903.

"At that time there were seven electric mules, or motor trucks, in the service. These motor trucks were fourteen feet long, were equipped with twin motors equal to eighty mule power. Retaining walls of stone were built along the canal in the city, tracks were laid and electric poles with the wires were put up. 'Turning bridges' were erected for the 'electric mule' at Twelfth street and Hartwell, and a large headquarters building was erected on the canal between Walnut and Main streets. Construction costs were reported to have exceeded a million and a half. On the trip that I made our boat was pulled up the canal at the normal rate of three to four miles an hour. As we reached the suburbs I saw several women working in truck gardens and wearing wooden shoes!"

But the advent of interurbans and of automobiles and other changes in the transportation field spelled the doom of the "electric mule."

Girl Is Saved! Oh, Glory! Now Read Rest of Story

"Life's darkest moment" for me came when I was given the job of seeing that a certain young lady, who had fallen into the water through a hole in the ice, got home at once; and there I was without even a nickel car fare. I started running her along to keep her from freezing, and when a Clifton-Ludlow car came by, I convinced her that her only safety consisted of keeping on running. On, on we ran, mile after mile, up the B. & O. tracks, and into Northside on the gallop. She changed to dry clothing and thanked me for being so "thoughtful" as to keep her running to get warm, so that she didn't even catch cold.

Unless she sees this in print, this girl, now a prominent Northside society leader, will never know the real reason why we ran all the way home that cold day instead of boarding the "jerky."

Those were the happy days.—Charles A. Smithner, 4414 Haight avenue, Northside.

"Sincerely Hope Boulevard Will Be Called Towpath"

Dear Mr. Ludwig: During vacation we often hiked out to "White Fence," where the water was clearer, and had trees to rest under, and where there was no danger of being chased by cops. That walk along the towpath used to be quite an event, and mother's bread and butter used to taste mighty good, when we reached home.

I sincerely hope that the boulevard will be called the Towpath, instead of Central Parkway.—Charles L. Weber, North Vernon, Ind.

Crowd Pushed Street Car Up Canal Bridge

Our crowd was a great help to Vine street car drivers. The mules couldn't pull the cars up the grade to the top of the Vine street canal bridge, and we would push them up, starting the car at Court street.—Morris H. Tobias, Pugh Building.

MULES WALKING ALONG "ELECTRIC MULE" TRACKS ON TOWPATH IN SUBURBS.

Whew! Forty Miles an Hour on the Old Canal!

Moses Strauss, ye managing editor, easily qualifies as a charter member of the Old Towpath Club.

He did forty miles an hour on the canal before the days of the automobile.

He did it on skates—at least it seemed like forty miles an hour in the era of horse-drawn street cars.

"When the ice in the canal downtown was broken up or melted from the hot water from plants along the shore, we would take a horse-car out to Carthage or some other place out of the city and have a grand skate," he reminisced. "And there was no barbecue or hot lunch stand every few feet as the motor traveler finds today. If a boy survived the rugged experiences along the canal he was apt to become a robust man."

Cool Drink, and Pretzels, and Dried Herring, Free!

The water came down Eggleston avenue in a millrun and turned the wheels of old man Fagin's flour mill and others. On a hot summer's day any of us could walk into Gerke's brewery on the canal bank and get a cool drink and lunch—pretzels and dried herring—free! Cunningham, Davis and Lippincott pork houses on Canal street. Cannon made at Greenwood foundry in Civil War.

Fine apple orchard near Mohawk and boys peppered with shot one day. And Kestner's fishing tackle store. Skillman's freight and passenger boats. Round trip to Dayton took a week—through most beautiful country. Goodby, old canal. We will always remember "Over the Rhine."—"R," 67, of 1706 Linn street.

This Explains How The Boulders Got Here!

About fifty-four years ago I rode on the canal boat Baltimore, owned by my father, Christian Huber, and driven by my sister. We hauled many a load of boulders for alleys and streets of Cincinnati, of which a few are left. Afterwards we located at Lesourdsville, O., and loaded ice boats for Cincinnati users.—Mrs. George Knapp, 501 Crawford street, Middletown, O.

Last Boy In Gets a Ducking!

The aqueduct and a place just below it, called the "Sandies," were our favorite swimming holes. We would go "out to the canal" nearly every day during vacation time; just a little gang of barefoot kids kicking our feet through the deep dust along the Carthage pike and down Mitchell avenue toward the canal. We used to hold that the last one in would receive a ducking, and in order to escape the ducking, and be the first one in, some of us would undress along Mitchell avenue and run the remainder of the way in the bathing suit nature provided for us. Of course we would kick up all the dust we could so as to render us invisible to the passerby. Our favorite sport was to dive over the railing of the aqueduct without touching it. Another of our pranks was to swim out and grab hold of the rudder of a passing canal boat, climb to the top and dive off. Those were the good old days.—Morton C. Ewing, 4112 Twenty-ninth street, Oakley.

Swimmer, Aged Ninety, Still Recalls Early Days

I was born on Wilder's Hill, now called Price Hill, in June, 1839. I fished, skated and swam in the old canal many, many times. I could tell you of many thrilling youthful combats and experiences we had in the good old days never to return.—Dock Wilder, 571 Elberon avenue.

SKATING ON THE CANAL—"ALL SHOD WITH STEEL WE HISSED ALONG THE POLISHED ICE."—PHOTO FROM MRS. LIDA W. BART.

"Whole Family Laughs Over Funny Stories"

"I and my five grown children are all eligible to join the Towpath Club," says Mrs. Sophie Behrle, 110 Baker avenue, St. Bernard. "My son Albert suffered a fractured ear drum swimming in the canal and all of the boys had great fun in the water. My daughters, too, played on the shore, fell in and were pulled out by the boys. We are all laughing over the funny stories in the Times-Star about the good old days. My brother, J. G. Springard, fell in the canal when the bridge at Walnut street collapsed during a big fire. Then he went to school with his wet clothes—and received a whipping, besides! My son Henry made the famous canal junket with the city and State officials from Cincinnati to Lockland on August 1, 1900. The governor, Mayor Fleischmann, Garry Herrmann and other notables were on the canal boat."

Pioneer Ice Cutter

Sig. Frietsch, of the Max Wocher & Sons Co., says: "My father was the first man to cut ice on the canal and invented a process of doing this—a patented rake to pull the ice out of the canal. The ice was used in the packing plants for refrigeration purposes."

Knorr Company Had Fleet of Iceboats

"We had a fleet of iceboats on the canal that brought ice from the lake to Lesourdesville, O., seven miles above Hamilton, to our Cincinnati icehouse," said Charles Knorr, formerly of the old Knorr Ice Company. "We had ten big icehouses on one side of the lake and two immense houses on the other. When there was a good ice harvest the supply would be enough for two years. The lake was fed from the waters of the Big Miami River."

Canal Boats Carried Train Passengers To Train Connections During Great Flood of '84

Frank P. Fish, Sr., former railroad conductor, of Ft. Mitchell, Ky., who loaned a picture like the one on the opposite page, writes that he was in charge of the canal boat during the flood of 1884. He adds: "During that great flood, when the railroad depots were under water, the canal and horse drawn vehicles offered the only method of transportation out of th ecity. This boat (of which I was in charge), and others, were chartered by the (then) Bee Line Railway for hauling passengers and mail between Sycamore street and St. Bernard. t also gave the passengers a wonderful view of the flooded district. Prior to obtaining the boats we ran through the ditch with water over the floor of the cars. Our first outside station was Eighth street, then Thomas street, Stock Yards and Winton Place. The water finally driving us to St. Bernard to mail rail connections."

Now Lives in Chicago, But Recalls Happy Canal Days!

One of the favorite tricks of some of the Mohawk gang was to cut a hole in the ice and cover it up with snow and slush and see some boy come along and go under the water. It was great sport to dry out your clothes by standing in front of the bonfire on the bank at "Second Basin." There were one or two old canal boats sunk in the basin and it was great fun to get up into one of them and dive off the side of the old boat, which was usually in clear water.—C. A. Benninger, 9049 South Robey street, Chicago.

He's a Hero After Our Own Heart!

Mr. Charles Ludwig:
I dove from shore to shore underneath empty sand boats.
But here is the thrill of a lifetime. I used to stand in the middle of the canal, wait for the moving canal boat, jump and catch the bow bumper, made of rope, climb to the top of the bow beam and dive off the beam while boat was moving to the front, come up and climb up to the top and dive off again and again. Can you beat it?
Let us name it the Towpath, a companion to the Bowery of New York, instead of Central Parkway.—Louis C. Hahn, Sr., Bridgetown, O.

Blockade of Boats Along Old Canal— One Stuck in Mud!

We could jump from our back porch at Brighton into the canal.
There used to be blockades of canal boats on the canal. A boat would get stuck, or spring a leak, and there would be boats for some distance. This blockade would last sometimes for days. Boats used to unload at Brighton—corn for the Duckworth Distillery, cord wood for the pork houses or bakeries, ice, sand, etc. There was a German family moved to Brighton with several children. One of the boys took his father's accordion to wash it in the canal. He dipped up and down several times, until it fell apart. All he had left was the strap handle!—Henry Schopper.

Swimming Teacher Towpath Product

Gustave L. Stecher, swimming teacher at Woodward High School, learned to swim in the canal. He writes:
Lou Ehrgott, the popular music teacher, was one of the best swimmers who gathered nightly for a swim with our crowd, back of old Music Hall, for there was the sand depot of the town, and the bottom of the canal was nice to stand on, and the sand on the bank was an additional attraction.

FLOOD OF '84 SUBMERGED STATIONS. PASSENGERS MADE TRAIN CONNECTIONS AT WINTON PLACE BY CANAL BOAT—PHOTOS LOANED BY LEVI GOODALE AND FRANK P. FISH, SR., FT. MITCHELL.

Sang His Way on Canal Boat From Cincinnati to Toledo

"It was like a trip around the world for me," said John L. Horgan, canal swimmer and skater, and managing director of the Hotel Sinton, in telling about his romantic boat ride on the canal from Cincinnati to Toledo when he was a boy.

He is the only member of the society who sang his way from one end of the canal to the other—some 250 miles across the State.

"My great canal trip was made over a third of a century ago," he said. "At the age of 7 I was already singing with the Fields & Dockstader Minstrels, and the next year, aged 8, I was instructed to join the Primrose & Dockstader Company at Toledo. I made the trip to Toledo via the canal boats, sang for the captains and boat people and had a wonderful time. It was like making a trip around the world, a romantic, delightful journey I shall never forget. I arrived safely at Toledo, joined the troupe and sang on the stage for eight more years before entering the hotel business."

Big Fire of 1874! Crowded Bridge Fell!

I was born on Court street in 1860 and my playground was the towpath. In 1874 I saw the Walnut street canal bridge collapse, filled with men and women on their way to work, watching the George Pelstring cigar box factory burning on the south side of the canal, two doors east of Walnut. There was a halfbreed Mexican known as Black Pete. He would come to the house at 4 o'clock in the morning and take me down to the canal where he had a two-seated sliding seat boat made of canvas and we would row out the canal beyond St. Bernard, where we would gather what he called blood root, to make a medicine.—J. E. Meyers, 1759 Cleneay avenue, Norwood.

From Sacramento, Cal.

I swam, on a dare, from Second Basin, back of the Refuge, to the Brighton house, without touching bottom. The water in those days was clear as crystal and the bottom was sandy.—John R. Lyon, Sacramento, Cal.

Canal Was My Atlantic Ocean!

Dear Mr. Ludwig: Great stuff—the Canal Swimmers' Society! The old canal was my Atlantic Ocean. As one of the old Oliver street crowd we lived on its banks.

Diving off the bridges from Main street to Liberty street was a real stunt. You did not know what you would come up with, sometimes tin cans, gasoline stoves, and occasionally old shoes.

Who remembers the old sand house at Oliver and Canal? Many a good tumbler was developed there. They had an old diving board and it was common for them to do a double somersault. There were a couple of old fellows, who told us they were clowns from Robinson's Circus, and came there to practice. We would dive into the canal, then into the sand, and then back into the canal for a wash.

There used to be a storekeeper on the corner of Canal and Main streets, who had a lot of skiffs, and who sold fishing tackle, nets and minnows. We used to take a skiff and a tub, row out to Second Basin and seine for minnows for him. Our pay was the ride in the skiff and it was some job, as we used to crowd in five or six of our pals.—Lou Fortwangler, Seventh and Race streets.

One of First Canal Factories

My great-grandfather and my grandfather (Mr. John Howard Ballance) built one of the first buildings on the canal.

In 1831 John Howard Ballance erected a factory (known then as 108 Canal, between Race and Vine) where he established the first wholesale wool business west of the Allegany Mountains. He also dealt in hides.—Lida Ballance, northwest corner Burton Woods lane and Clinton Springs avenue, Avondale.

New Pump for Our Boat!

My father, John H. Fannich, made the lamps they used on the canal boats. They were large and square, with a glass case, and they had three reflectors. He also made the hand pumps they used to pump the water out of the boats.—Clara Fannich Holmes.

PLAYMATES OF THE TOWPATH 79

All dressed in white,
On a Sunday bright,
What jolly fun
To speed right through
Camp Washington!

—PHOTO LOANED BY F. L. TULLIS.

Boat Had Unique Propellers

Col. William T. Johnston of the Johnston Machinery Company tells of a unique canal boat he helped to provide with machinery in the nineties.

"This was an ordinary canal boat driven in a most unusual way—by gasoline power applied to two screw-wheels, one on each side of the boat, just off the mid-section," said Col. Johnston. "William C. Lomb of Covington was the inventor and I furnished the driving machinery. Each driving wheel was cylindrical in shape, with a spiral screw-propeller partly submerged. I took a trip on the boat up the canal and it worked all right, though it never came into general use because of the advent of the electric mule and other developments."

Champion Crawfish Catcher Had Pipe Organ on Canal!

In 1858 I went to Twelfth and Plum under the bridge and caught so many crawfish I could hardly carry them home. I boiled them and we ate until the boys had plenty. I bought a pleasure boat thirty years ago, twenty feet long, and cruised up the canal to Toledo and back. The music was a pipe organ—some music. Pete Renner, John Ragan, Frank Ratterman, Jakey Hughes, Add Krippner, William Krippner, Ed Sternberger, Allen Omeyers and Robert Miller were in the party. When the Queen City Fishing Club camped at Woodsdale we built a pontoon bridge over the canal so we could get across to our camp.—Frank Krippner, 3231 Brotherton road.

Forbidden To Go In Canal—So He Fell In!

"Thirty-five years ago I had my first dip in the canal at Elder street. I was forbidden to go in the water, but while standing on the bank watching the other boys with a longing desire to be in with them and at the same time watching the sun's reflection in the water became dizzy and fell in the water. So that was the beginning of my canal pleasures.—H. W. Shoup, Dayton, Ky.

News from Veteran Canal Swimmer, Aged 90

From Fred Runk, Sr., 90 years old: Arrived in Cincinnati in 1849 from Toledo, via Miami Canal, a journey of eight days. Remembers canal water being as clear as crystal and was their drinking water during entire trip. Recalls swimming in the canal at 12 years. At that time there also was a covered wooden bridge at Liberty street. Swam at Fourteenth street when Cincinnati orphan asylum was there on Music Hall site. Has lived on Pleasant stree. seventy-nine years.

Fished With a Wash-Boiler! And Caught a Red-Horse!

I caught red-horse fish with a wash-boiler at Second Basin. How many of the old boys are left that would start at Sycamore street bridge and jump from each bridge until they hit Mohawk, and then would have to run the gantlet of all the gangs until he hit his gang at Fifteenth street? Some days, happy days.—William Sanders, 3333 Graydon avenue.

Hundreds Leaped In At Stroke of Bell!

About 1870 I was a regular member of the Canal Swimmers and would go in swimming every night. Our place was between Main and Walnut streets. We used to sit on the pile of flasks used for molding purposes. At 8 o'clock the bell would ring and instantly we kids dove in like a lot of frogs. It was a great sight as over a hundred went in at that square on a hot night.—Fred Wiebking.

Her Playmate, at Five, Lived on Canal Boat

When driving along Central Parkway, many happy memories come back to me. I see a little girl of five, playing with another little girl, who lived on a canal boat which was stopping near the Fourteenth street bridge for two weeks. I was in and out of that boat, where living quarters were so tiny and so clean that I imagined it a play house. And when the boat was ready to move on, I was broken-hearted, and wanted to go along. The father of the little girl and owner of the boat said I could. Without permission from home I went, and when the boat neared the Fifteenth street bridge he lifted me up from the deck and, setting me on the bridge, said: "Now, run home." Which I did.—Emma Werner Dollman, 411 Harrison avenue, Cheviot.

Joe Schenke, on Gondola, Made Canal Welkin Ring!

I took part in "Marco Polo," the beautiful show given on the canal bank. Remember the beautiful sight of the gondola? Lighted and decorated, gliding up the canal, to the melody of Mascagni's Intermezzo, "Cavalliera Rusticana," sung by Mr. Joseph Schenke, Cincinnati's well-known tenor. I was cellist.

The director at the Keith-Albee Theater today, Rudolph Tschudi, violinist, also took part in the Marco Polo show and rode in the gondola.

Now while motoring along our beautiful boulevard, I long to ride between Twelfth street and Music Hall and live in those dear memories of years gone by.—Dr. William F. Supper, Iris avenue, Kennedy Heights.

"Cop" Rode Great White Steed!

I can still see Officer Booth mounted on his great and famous white police horse (there was no smarter horse in those days), prancing up and down the old towpath yelling at us kids to come out of the water, where he could get hold of us. But we would invariably leave the water on the opposite bank! I remember my brother Will's last sw.m in the old canal—he dived off a canal boat into the bank, was rendered unconscious, and had to have fifteen stitches put in his scalp.—Louis Botzung.

Canal Falls in Woodland, with Clifton Castles Above, Millcreek Below, Scene of Rare Beauty

Here are the beautiful waterfalls of the canal—one of the most picturesque and charming scenes that graced the entire towpath.

The Canal Scribe visited the scene the other day and, though the canal bed was dry and filled with grass and underbrush, the falls still were there! Enough rain had fallen and frozen to re-create these beautiful falls!

The heavy masonry and stonework of the falls remain undamaged and all who love beautiful scenery will enjoy a visit to the "falls," even though the water no longer flows over them. The falls were created by the overflow from the canal. They were located in a setting of rare loveliness, on the hillside below the famous ivy-towered castles of Clifton. The falls were situated just below the fine castle that is now Scarlet Oaks Hospital. A few feet above the falls the canal flowed through a woodland. The falls were in a delightful glen with a forest on both sides. The excess water from the canal, after leaping over the falls, rollicked down the hill-slope under the railroad and into Millcreek, just below. Creek, falls, hillside, canal and the castles above made a memorable picture.

The picture above was taken by W. H. Boone. The falls were a favorite sketching place for Frank Wilmes and other artists, and years ago an Indian—"Indian Joe"—lived there in the woods.

The falls were opposite Spring Grove Cemetery and back of the interurban depot on Spring Grove avenue, and can be reached by way of the wooden bridge over Millcreek near the depot.

Thousands have gone swimming at the falls and Mr. Wilmes, Henry Ruhstaller and others loaned us photos of the scene.

W. E. Weghorst writes from Reading, Pa., that he saw the falls picture in the Times-Star and it brought back delightful memories of the falls and the ivy-covered stone house near by, in which he lived years ago. He adds:

I can recall many of the pleasures spent at the old swimming holes, as well as remember how artists would spend the entire Sunday with brush and easel painting pictures of the waterfalls and the beautiful old ivy-covered stone house.

We used to catch crawfish and cook them in an old tomato can beside the old waterfalls. As I think of those days I can still hear the roar of the water coming over the falls and seem to hear the voice of "Old Indian Joe," who used to spend some time in the woods at the falls.

While I write these lines the radio is playing "Carry Me Back to Old Virginia," but it should be to the old swimming hole in good old Cincinnati. I recall swimming in the canal above the waterfalls, how we boys used to catch the sand boats, climbing up the front end, jumping down into the sand, then diving off the rear, where we always expected a good ducking of ice water by the man at the rudder. One night while swimming a sand boat was approaching, so, hailing my buddies by their "old nicknames" we climbed on the boat. Unfortunately, I was in lead. I dropped down into the hull. Instead of finding the usual sand I found myself in the midst of a "moonlight" picnic of young men and women. Being in my natural bathing suit, you can imagine my embarrassment as I ran the full length of the boat amid cheers from the picnickers, received my ducking of ice water, then dove off the rear.

We had our skiffs and canoes and enjoyed the beautiful scenery, which words can not describe. We would pass the waterfalls, then the old Statehouse, where we usually found the State boat, in charge of Capt. Irwin, tied up across the canal, but which always was pushed clear of the bank as a boat approached to permit its passage. As we rowed along we saw the usual familiar fishermen with their dough bait sitting along the bank with their trotlines of sixteen to thirty hooks, protected from the sun by the massive silver poplars.

The croaking frogs, the mules and boats, the boatman blowing his trumpet, and the quiet flowing water are all gone! The boys of today can never appreciate what the dear old canal meant to the boys of generations past. "Gone are the days, but old memories linger on."

And George Lane, now of Lawrenceburg, Ind., writes:

Dear Mr. Ludwig: I often swam at the falls of the canal. We used to go in at the lower step, back in behind the falls, and the water rolled in front of us in a roaring mass. I recollect an old one-legged man we boys called Indian Joe. Each summer for several years Indian Joe would camp at the falls. I have seen him fish for crawfish with a chunk of bacon, cut the tails off and boil them over a fire. Also catch chubs—and we boys used to bring him things from home, one a cup of sugar, another some coffee, and another his pocket full of potatoes. He said he was an Indian chief and had several tintypes of Indian girls who were his daughters.

William N. Hirst writes of the thrill of swimming in the falls, saying: "As a Cumminsville boy I went nearly every week day or night to swim in the old canal near the falls. And what a thrill it was to go down to the lowest fall and get behind that sheet of water and try to yell so as to be heard above its thunder;"

"Over-the-Rhine"

Harry J. Levi, president of the Central Avenue Business Men's Association:

Forty years ago I crossed the canal a thousand times on my way Over-the-Rhine, when Cincinnati was a wide-open town. In those days traveling salesmen would ride 100 to 150 miles on a Saturday to spend the week-end in Cincinnati.

Fell In, Held Onto Money!

Fifty years ago, when I was six, my mother sent me to the butcher store at Mohawk and I walked on the canal ice until I fell in. I was almost drowned. A man rescued me just in the nick of time —but I held onto the meat money in my hand through all my struggles in the water!—John Fath, Northside.

CANAL FALLS FROZEN, 1907—PHOTO FROM EARL BLERSCH.

Earliest Picture Shows Plant Operated By Canal Water Power for Seventy-five Years

The earliest industrial canal boat picture found by the Canal Scribe is seen on the opposite page. It shows a small, old-fashioned canal boat in front of Pearce's factory at what is now the northeast corner of Fifth street and Eggleston avenue. Frank Atkins, of the Atkins & Pearce Company, which is still in the cotton manufacturing business on the same site, loaned the picture and said: "Our business dates back to 1817 and I think we moved to the canal bank on Eggleston avenue in the '40s. The picture dates back to around 1845. Part of the old building is still standing and used by us. Just above the main building, in the picture, may be seen the overflow from a canal lock and the lock buildings. From this point the water had a drop of ten feet, turning our water wheels. The water came out of the tunnel at the north end of our building and flowed back into the canal in front of our place. The semicircular top of the tunnel is visible in the picture—and the tunnel exists to this day in our cellar. We used this power for operating our machinery for about seventy-five years—till the canal went dry in 1919."

Rescued, He Writes Acrostic!

I dove, cut my head on a broken bottle, was nearly drowned and was going down for the third time when rescued. I heard the most wonderful symphony as I was going under. They rolled me on a barrel and got most of the water out of me, and I got a licking, besides, when I reached home! I'll close with this acrostic:

The yesterdays have passed us by,
How much we miss them, you and I
Each know, when summer's heat is nigh!

Or when the skating season's near,
Long pent-up dreams of yesteryear
Draw for us pictures filled with cheer.

The old canal was like a thread
Of silver, from a Land of Oz,
Which by dream fairy fingers spread,
Painted new life where hope had fled,
And brought to us a world that was—
The Towpath, for its civic fame,
Has our indorsement for a name.

   A. FRANK HOFFMANN,
    3669 Stettinius avenue.

Swam at "White Fence!"

The White Fence was the best place along the canal to swim. No fear of "Cheese it! The cop!" for there were no homes, only factories, in this neighborhood—where the Jacob Vogel packing house now is. A pear orchard was close by.—J. B. Wetterer.

Anybody Find This Girl's Silk Umbrella?

"As little girls, Myra Ward, Celia Gorman and I, calling ourselves the St. Clair Sisters, used to conduct a juvenile theater on the canal bank at Main street," writes Gussie Nadler Voss, Alexandria, Ky. "We put on some fine shows, and drew crowds—free.

"On my sister Minnie's birthday we decided on a skiff ride. Her sweetheart had given her a silk umbrella with a gold handle. After we were all ready to go one of the men at Kestner's, where we rented the skiff, gave us a start. He pushed the skiff and upset the crowd in the canal. We were all in white starched dresses! Down went the new umbrella! The boys dove for hours for it, but had no success. I wonder if they found it when they drained the canal?"

"Cops" Rushed Out Rear Doors of Factory!

I still have scars on my head from diving. I recall some very narrow escapes from the cops while swimming in the rear of Maescher's packing house, where the cops came out of the rear doors of the packing house, and were right on us.

Several times my mother had to go to the station house with me to get my clothes after several of us had eluded the cops.—Wonderful days!—John Roth, 3351 McFadden avenue.

CANAL, BOAT AND LOCKS, FIFTH AND EGGLESTON, IN 1840's—OLDEST CANAL SCENE—LOANED BY FRANK ATKINS.

"We'd Be Arrested for Speeding if Our Launch Made More Than Ten Miles An Hour"

All aboard for a ride on the famous old steam launch, shown on the opposite page and built by Frank and William Ernst in 1889 for Sunday pleasure outings on the canal.

"She could easily make ten miles an hour!" writes Frank Ernst, 716 East Epworth avenue. "If we went faster we would be arrested for speeding!—and for washing the banks. The boat was twenty-five feet long, and on our pleasure trips we would carry twenty-two people, including the band and one-half barrel. Sometimes we carried a grind organ that sounded like a calliope! We would stop at every brewery on the canal, serenade the boss, go on to Hamilton and return. Several times our keg rolled off the back seat into the water—and the man in charge of it would jump right in after the keg and rescue it. Sometimes we would tow boys and girls along in a skiff to hear them sing."

The picture was taken at the Walnut street bridge. George E. Ernst, son of Frank, also writes telling of his happy canal days, and concludes: "Oh, I wish I could dream, some night, of my childhood days on the canal!"

Congressman Hess Has Perfect Canal Record

Here is Congressman William E. Hess's perfect record as a Canal Swimmer:

"I was born near Mohawk bridge, swam in and skated on the canal almost as soon as I was able to walk, owned a flatboat, caught carp and mudcats at Second Basin and used to jump on the canal boats from the bridges."

"Happiness Now Complete!"

From William Reehl, former president of the Cincinnati Club:

"I belong to every kind of a club in the world except a canal society, and now my happiness is complete.

"I fished in the canal when there were no fish in it. I swam in the canal when it contained lots of mud and scarcely any water, and I skated on the canal when it had ice so thin that I went through."

Captain of Mud Digger!

Here's a Mohawker, canal swimmer, skiff owner. Also took care of George B. Cox's state boat and the old mud digger one winter.—Fred Sandman, Cheviot.

Rolled Big Waves of Water From Aqueduct to Street

Greg O'Leary's crowd made the canal their "playground, gymnasium and amusement park" and they explored every foot of the towpath from Cheapside to Second Basin.

"I learned the art of swimming in just one lesson," O'Leary writes. "The boys just dropped me off the Sycamore street bridge—and told me to swim to shore. And I did! Fought my way to the bank! It was one of the greatest thrills of my life.

"A favorite stunt was for the whole gang to go in where the canal passed over Mitchell avenue and all hang on the edge. By swaying in unison we could roll the water over the edge. By timing this roll we managed to roll plenty over the side just as an old-time open summer car was passing below. Can you imagine those sheiks of 1905-06 hanging four deep on the running board all dolled up in peg-top pants—the sun beating down and all bright and merry—then have a cloudburst of canal water hit them, curl up their straw hats and take all the trick creases out of those coats and trousers?"

Ice at Lesourdsville Lake!

Alice M. Voorheed, 129 West Third street, Covington, sent in pictures of the lake at Lesourdsville, on the canal, "where the big Knorr ice houses used to be."

READY FOR SUNDAY OUTING, 1889—BAND TUNED, FLAGS FLYING, STEAM UP! LOANED BY FRANK ERNST.

> **Towpath Heroes We Here Loud-Pedal!**
> **All Are Brave, But Only One Has Medal!**

This is a chapter for Heroes!

Heroes of the Canal Swimmers' Society!

Many deeds of splendid courage and valor, of bravery and intrepidity were performed on the banks of the placid old stream.

A boy of 8 is knocked unconscious in the water—drawn by suction under a canal boat! Fred Hornberger dives into the icy water and brings up the almost lifeless form of the lad, who is now Theodore Hahn, Jr., popular musical director of the Albee-Libson theaters in Cincinnati.

A great dog falls through the ice and is drowning! Harry Pugh, president of the A. H. Pugh Printing Company, hears the plaintive moans of the dog, takes off his skates and shoes and at the risk of his own life leaps into the hole with the dog, suffers and freezes—but saves the creature.

A child has sunk to the bottom of the wintry canal! Ben Simkin, schoolboy, bursts through the crowd, dives in the middle of the canal where the child was last seen, saves its life and receives a medal!—so far as known, the only medal awarded a canal hero.

No, it was the second decoration, for when Donald Copelan, aged 6, was rescued from drowning he bestowed upon his rescuer his mother's G. A. R. auxiliary badge!

The Rev. Howard Melish distinguished himself by boldly diving into the icy water to save a dog.

E. H. Hey, Avondale, saved two boys. Joseph Feldman tried to save a dog and had to be rescued himself from the frigid water—his clothes were frozen stiff on him.

Charles Keith was rescued twice, with a pole each time!

Tip Nightingale's wife was all but gone when a canal boatman, seeing her hair, rescued her!

A water spaniel should know how to swim, but Jack Hagedorn's didn't—so it was up to Jack to jump in and save his dog, and he did it.

> **Pugh Risked Life to Save Drowning Dog**
>
> Harry Pugh, president of the A. H. Pugh Printing Company, risked his life to save a dog in December, 1916. The dog, a fine, large St. Bernard, belonging to F. W. Boye, Jr., Greendale avenue, Clifton, broke through a small hole in the ice at Mt. Storm, Clifton. He tried hard and long to climb out, but was unable to do so, gave up and moaned as if dying. Pugh, who had been skating with a party, took off his skates and shoes—so as to be able to swim better—and leaped into the icy waters to save the exhausted, drowning canine. Pugh seized the dog by the collar and swam to the shore with him, breaking the ice as he swam. Pugh, soaked in icy water, was unable to put on his shoes again. He ran barefooted on the snow to keep warm—but his feet were partly frozen. A hot bath and stimulants later helped him recuperate.

Quietly, without haste or excitement, the canal boat passes by. A happy boy stands alone on the towpath at the left and gazes on contentedly. When the boat has passed he waves a farewell to the helmsman, resting at the rear of the boat under an awning with a hand on the rudder lever. The water is placid. It is a summer afternoon. The banks of the canal are lined with trees, and many birds fill the air with cheery song. The tramp of the plodding, patient mules grows fainter in the distance. All is serene and peaceful along the old stream. This scene was back of Clifton. The photo was loaned by J. R. Pigman.

JUMPED OFF BRIDGE; SAVED LITTLE BOY

Dr. W. H. Mueller, Orlando, Fla., formerly of Fifteenth and Race streets, delivering a bottle of medicine for his father, saved a boy from drowning in the canal—but lost the bottle of medicine.

"Crossing the Fourteenth street canal bridge to deliver the medicine, I was startled by the screams of a child who had fallen into the canal. Canal-bridge jumping was my trade in those days—I slipped through the bars of the bridge, hung, dropped into the shallow water and mud, and carried the boy out. I did not swim out with him—the water was not deep enough. I carried the boy home—and his father tried to beat me with a bat! I returned to the bridge for my medicine bottle—but alas it was gone!"

Valorous Maiden Saved Her Brother

And here we have the case of a brave young sister who saved her brother. Miss Genevieve L. King, 2204 Drex avenue, Norwood, joins the Canal Swimmers' Society, with her brother, and tells the story. She writes:

"One dark wintry night, when the old towpath was slightly covered with ice, my brother and I were returning from a theater (one of those where we could sit in a seat, two for one nickel). Well, brother insisted upon trying out the ice, just along the edge, of course. He became bolder and ventured further, with disastrous results! He fell in, was partly submerged beneath the ice! Then I came to the rescue and pulled him out and took off my raincoat, wrapped it around his legs so he wouldn't catch cold. My, but it was a cold night!"

Rescue Dove! Stuck in Mud!

One of the grandchildren of Dick Painer, the deputy sheriff of Hamilton County, fell in the canal and Dick made a dive for him and he stuck in the mud (head first, ha, ha!) and, as luck happened, someone was there to pull Dick out by his feet, and also saved the child. Those were the good old days.—Mrs. Phil C. Hirlinger, 5001 Hamilton avenue.

Saw Girl's Bright Red Hair! And Rescued Her!

A girl who was skating ahead of me went through the ice. She was going at such speed she went through the thin ice and under the thicker ice. I pulled her out by her hair. If it had not been of such a vivid color, red, I would have had a much harder job rescuing her.—Harry E. Fisk, 6259 Cary avenue.

Ben Simkin Awarded Medal for Heroism!

Ben Simkin, 3585 Van Antwerp place, is, so far as known, the only Cincinnatian ever to receive formal recognition in the form of a medal for bravery in saving life on the canal.

When Ben was about 12 years old, going home from the Sixth District School on Elm street, he noticed a crowd standing on the canal bank. "A little boy has drowned!" was the cry raised.

Ben brushed his way through the crowd to the edge of the canal and the crowd pointed to the spot in the middle where they had seen some commotion a moment before and where the little boy—named Ben Nedelman—had disappeared from view. The Nedelman child had been jostled into the canal while playing on the shore.

It was winter weather and the water was cold. Ben Simkin quickly threw off his coat and hat and leaped into the water. He swam to the place pointed out, dove to the bottom, found the unconscious form of the little boy, brought it to the surface and swam to shore with it. The child was revived after much difficulty. Ben modestly walked away. His gallantry was reported to a health commission that awarded him a medal for bravery, and this medal was formally presented to him by Judge Robert Marx at a meeting in the Jewish Center. Simkin still has the medal.

How Alter Was Rescued

"I was nearly drowned in Ross's Basin," said Franklin Alter, Jr., 3006 Fairfield avenue. "Swimming there as a boy I became exhausted and was unable to reach the shore. I screamed and had gone down three times. Thanks to the quick and brave action of Harry Weaver, my life was saved. He was a strong swimmer. He threw off his shoes, coat and hat, swam out to where I sank, dove down, brought me up to the surface and swam with me to the shore.

"I recall swimming in the canal in February! It was a day of record-breaking warmth for that time of the year."

PULLED OUT OF ICE

Joseph A. Feldman, 3728 Spring Grove avenue, tells how he was saved after he had tried to rescue a dog: "When a boy about 7 years old, I fell into the canal running after a balloon, and one cold winter day I fell through the thin ice trying to save a dog. When the men pulled me out my clothes were frozen on me. I still recall the name of one of the men—Ralph Dill. They built a bonfire and tried to dry my clothes. One of the coopers ran into the distillery and brought a bottle of what was known in those days as high wine and the men rubbed me with it to protect me from catching cold."

Rescued Two Boys!

One day a policeman on the west side of the canal wanted me to come over and be arrested. I had nothing on and my clothes were at his feet. I ran home to Fifteenth and Elm streets without a stitch of clothes on and got a good beating.

Many a day after school I helped unload sand boats, and about 5 o'clock rode on the canal boat to Clifton bridge and walked home to Fifteenth and Elm streets and received nothing for my labor—but those were fine days for me. I often dove from the Fourteenth street bridge and sometimes stuck in the mud. I saved two lives in the canal. One about 100 feet south of the bridge and the other at Fourteenth street.—E. H. Hey, Avondale.

About Life Saving And Cannon Balls

While swimming at Twelfth street I saw something which looked like a clump of grass and I grabbed it and found it was the head of a young boy who was drowning. I dragged him ashore, where ice men worked with him and brought him to life. I remember during the Civil War seeing them ship cannon balls on the canal boats.—Henry R. Wellman, 28 East McMillan.

ON A CLEAR SUNDAY. THE CANAL, LOOKING EAST FROM PLUM STREET—FRANK WILMES PHOTO.

Rev. Melish Rescued His Drowning Dog!

The most thrilling and heroic deed that I ever witnessed was the saving of a dog's life.

The Rev. William Howard Melish, who formerly lived in Clifton, rescued his dog from an icy grave.

Some one threw a stick out on the thin ice of the canal at Mummert's basin. The dog went after it and broke through and swam and swam around in a circle, his weight breaking the ice as he tried to crawl up on the ice. Finally Mr. Melish deliberately jumped into the canal and lifted him out. Mr. Melish and his dog were taken home in a carriage.—C. T. Russell.

Newsboy Saved Two!

"Times-Star Newsboy Saves Brother and Sister from Drowning!" So read a Times-Star headline twenty-eight years ago. D. J. Davis, 616 Vine street, leaped in and saved Mary and Gerald Schmidt, 4 and 6, who had fallen in the water near Fourteenth street. "Spectators on the bank let down an old rope from the bridge and towed the three of us to shore with it," writes Davis.

A Brave Life Saver!

Art Schuller, who lived around Wade street, saved so many boys from drowning in the canal that he was known as The Life Saver. I was tossed into the canal because I refused to get a dime's worth of beer for some men. I came out of the canal blue—my new blue knickers faded and colored my skin! I then did the errand and hurried back so fast that I stumbled and spilled the beer! Then I was thrown into the canal again!—Arthur George Wern, 1755 Harrison avenue.

Five Cents Saved Him!

Fifty years ago, while walking along the canal, I noticed a small fish that I tried to catch with a basket. I took hold of a towline fastened to a boat and reached out, but too far, and as this line was very slack I plunged head first into the canal. Were it not for that nickel I put into my mouth I might have drowned. Five-cent pieces those days were big money.—J. E. Fulweiler.

Saved Water Spaniel!

Jack Hagedorn, 1639 Marlowe avenue, writes: "Steve Brodie took a chance and so did my water spaniel dog and myself. I often skated and swam in the canal at Winton Place. One day at the age of ten the dog and I went swimming the first time—for the dog, not me. Well, to make a long story short, the dog jumped in after a stick I had thrown in and it was up to me to get him out after he had gone under twice, and remember, it was a water spaniel!"

Saved Lives of Two!

In 1886 I rescued a boy from drowning at Jackson street and the headline in the paper next day said: "Col. Deitsch should award this boy with a gold medal"—but I never received one. In 1887 I jumped in at Clay street and saved another child that was drowning.—William F. Rehse, Charlton street.

Rescued Her Niece!

At Walnut street my little niece fell in the canal and I plunged into the water to rescue her. Her coat formed a floating medium, keeping her on the surface. So, after wading some twenty feet with the water to my neck, for she floated in the middle of the canal, I towed her back to the bank and managed to lift her on land. The niece is Mrs. Fred J. Hoffmann, at that time Sallie Reemelin, daughter of Dr. R. H. Reemelin, my brother.—Lulu Reemelin, Norwood.

Tragedy on Canal

Years ago I leaped into the canal and pulled out a drowning boy. I recall the tragic death of a well-known sausage manufacturer, who, in a moment of despair, drowned himself in the canal. "Big Jimmy," a giant in stature, pulled a printer out of the canal one day, but the rescued man jumped in later again and succeeded in ending his life.—Arnold Reif.

I traveled by canal from Cincinnati to Toledo years ago. How many remember when Mr. Moore took the newsboys and bootblacks to Clifton Basin for a picnic?—Fred Grimmer.

CLUBHOUSE OF CLIFTON CANOE CLUB.

Charles P. Stamm of Wyoming, O., loaned the above photograph of the clubhouse of the Clifton Canoe Club. He says the house, located at Dietz's Basin, Clifton, was built from the wreckage of an old ice house there. Stamm was treasurer of the club and an ardent canal swimmer, skater, fisherman and canoeist. He would make extensive canoe trips—up the canal to the Big Miami, down the Big Miami to the Ohio, down the Ohio to Louisville—and then back up on the steamer, and up the canal to the clubhouse. He writes:

"I rode on the electric mules, on sand and freight boats, paddled canoes, rode on George Gano's steam launch, called the "Yadnus" (which is Sunday spelled the wrong way), shot snakes that were coiled on piles, and do hereby nominate myself to the most exalted position of chief snake shooter. Those were the days—long gone, never to return, but the memories linger on."

Iowa Gets "Kick" Out of Canal Yarns!

I am a Times-Star reader and sure get a great kick out of the Canal Society.

I did some skating and swimming in the canal, too. Those were the days, and to read of such things brings many a memory back to me.

The old towpath might be gone now, but let's keep the Canal Swimmers' Society living forever.—George Carlson, Cedar Rapids, Ia.

"Canal As Thrilling To Me As Ocean Trips"

"I have crossed the Atlantic ten times and have taken swims in the mighty oceans of the world—the Pacific and Atlantic—but these experiences were no more thrilling to me than was that of sitting barefooted on the canal bank as a child and splashing my feet in that wonderful waterway!"

So writes Elizabeth Hottendorf, 810 Richmond street. "And later—the wonderful, perfect day of skating."

"Shinny on Own Side," Played With Beer Bungs

Glad to join the club, as I learned swimming and skating in the old canal fifty years ago. When the canal was frozen over we would have a great game of "shinny on your own side" with old beer barrel bungs, between Main and Sycamore streets, and the banks on both sides would be lined with people watching us play and seeing how many of us would get hit with the bung.—Phil F. Harten, 533 East Southern avenue, Covington, Ky.

Ice-Breaker Broke Hearts!

"Remember the ice-breaker that crushed the ice in the canal and spoiled the skating?" writes Les Herbert Dinkelaker, 1614 Westmoreland avenue.

"Those who fished at Second Basin will remember the 'Basin Skinner.' This character was a mild old man who came every bright morning to fish. Always at the same spot, always with the same equipment: a cane pole, a can of worms and some dough bait. Rarely did he speak. If anyone caught any fish, it was the 'Basin Skinner.'"

Free Access to Tap Room!

The frontispiece of this book brought interesting recollections to Gregory S. Stewart, canal swimmer and well-known business man. "It shows the Plum street bend, where my father had his planing mill," said Stewart. "I joined him there in 1874. The picture shows the Schaller-Gerke brewery at the bend. I used to have free access to the tap room of that brewery because we used to cut up beech wood into shavings at our mill for the brewery. The shavings were used to settle beer."

There was the two-foot-away rule around Elder street and when I stood on the bank, two feet from the water, this rule permitted another boy to push me in—which he did! Then my clothes were dried at the hot-air fan of a nearby laundry! It was great!—Stanley J. Mohr, 197 Center street, Bellevue.

"I swam many times—till the body of a dead woman came up near me," says Charles Toedt.

Shipped Canal Lumber Forty-Six Years Ago

H. J. Doppes, president, J. B. Doppes Sons Lumber Company:

My father used to buy white pine lumber at Toledo and Sandusky, and it was shipped by canal boat.

At that time I was driving a horse and wagon for my father and I hauled lumber from the canal in 1872 and 1873. It did not pay to ship lumber by canal; the tally at this end fell short of the tally at the point of shipment.

Down by Old Millside— Miller Pulled Out Bodies!

Dear Sir: I think I qualify to be a member of the Canal Boys. My chief swimming hole seventy years ago was at Greenwood's Foundry, Canal and Walnut, and many a time I posed as "September Morn," with my clothes under my arm, racing up Walnut street to Hackman & Duesterberg's livery stable. Hiding in a horse's stall to get dressed, of course the wardrobe was quickly donned. Pair of pants and shirt —"that's all." I ran the Canal Mills for five years and the Root's Mill, now Dow's wholesale house, by water power. My men also pulled several dead men and women out on Cheapside, and so many dead babies, too.—William Rieker.

Fifty years ago a lad dove in the canal at Charlotte street and never came up. George Schlemmer dove down and brought up the boy—his head was stuck in the mud and he was drowned. We rolled him on the towpath to revive him, but in vain, for he was dead.—John Wartmann, 706 Center street, Bellevue, Ky.

Deserters Captured in '63 In a Boat on Canal!

I swam in the canal in 1862-63. I witnessed the capturing of several deserters of the Civil War. They were trying to escape in a boat on the canal, but were captured by guards at the Mohawk bridge. I helped build a bonfire along the canal to celebrate the fall of Richmond in 1865.—A Reader.

Like This Everywhere? It Was Not!
This Was a Towpath Garden Spot!

RASCHIG SCHOOL FLOWER GARDENS—PHOTO LOANED BY FELIX J. KOCH.

Here was a little beauty spot in the downtown section of the canal—the flower garden in front of the old Tenth District School, later named the Raschig School.

H. H. Raschig, one of Cincinnati's best-known school principals, was in charge at the Raschig School for over a third of a century. Thousands of Canal Swimmers came under his tutelage. Principal and pupils co-operated in planting the flower garden. Mayor Murray Seasongood, as a boy, attended the Old Tenth.

The late Principal Raschig's son, Frank L. Raschig, was chief engineer of the Rapid Transit Commission and planned the subway and boulevard along the towpath along which he, too, played as a lad.

The First Women Members!

Miss Sophie M. Collman, in charge of the Art Department of the Public Library and an enthusiastic research worker in canal history and art, and Mrs. Olive L. Koehler, 1810 Race street, were the first women to join the Canal Society. Miss Collman rode on the canal gondolas during one of the fall festival Venetian shows. Mrs. Koehler rode to Cincinnati to have her daguerreotype taken, years ago when a child of seven, on the canal boat Laurel, owned by her uncle and pictured in this book.

"One day I dove in and came up with a crock on my head!" writes Christ Toedt, 1862 Denham street.

Honeymoon on Canal!

My husband and I spent our honeymoon on a boating and camping trip on the canal. Our two daughters insisted on playing daily in the canal when only three years old. They fell in and whippings could not keep them away.—Mr. and Mrs. James Lanter.

Father Owned Canal Boat

In 1868 my father, Frederick Hornberger, had a canal boat with Capt. John Kuentzel in charge. It went to Lockland and carried farmers' products to Cincinnati — cord wood, food, eggs, feathers, hickory wood, butter—and these were sold very cheaply here.—Miss Minnie Hornberger.

Wedding Trip to Sandusky on Canal

Dear Mr. Ludwig:

I remember the old canal, when the banks were fresh and green with clean grass, and often bright with flowers, in the days before the Civil War.

I was a little girl then and my uncle, Samuel H. Taft, lived near the Plum street elbow of the canal, down where the boulevard now swings in a majestic curve.

What fun we used to have, throwing sticks and stones into the water, and watching the canal boats.

One day I remember with especial vividness. That was the time we took apples from the barge loaded for market; we were caught and got some plain and fancy spankings. Then, of course, I remember quite well when I was married to Alfred Korte, and we took a wedding trip on a canal boat all the way up to Sandusky, O.

The canal was clean and beautiful then.

MRS. BELLE TAFT KORTE,
1641 Sycamore Street.

He Had a Nice Hobby!

Many a time I was swimming in the old canal and somebody threw my clothes in. My hobby was to hang from the old Fifteenth street bridge and drop into a sand barge as it was passing by. When they chased us off we simply jumped in the old canal and swam ashore.—Canal Swimmer.

When Cows Fell In

I swam in the old canal in the summers of 1865 to 1869, and skated on it in the winters.

Once in a while I went swimming in the canal at Carthage. A drove of cows, while crossing the old wooden bridge at Cook street, proved too heavy a load for the structure, and down came the bridge, cows and all into the canal. Luckily, none were drowned.—Thomas B. Punshon, 2844 May street.

Dr. William C. Herman—Swam, skated and spent much of my time as a boy on its banks in the study of birds. This was east of Glendale.

She Caught a Fish— And Spanking, Too!

After recalling some of my experiences at the old Brighton swimming hole, my wife wanted to know where the women came in, in this society. She says she inherited the fishing fever, and wandered away from home many a time, toward the canal to try her skill as a fisherman. Remembers, on one especial occasion, after being all cleaned up by mother, went to the canal to fish but lost her balance and fell in. Someone pulled her out and she ran home, only to face a good spanking, all through which she held on to the fish!—Mr. and Mrs. Frank Faller, 3459 Alta Vista avenue, Cheviot.

Negroes Baptized in Canal

Interesting was the baptizing of the Negroes in Cumminsville at the place called Baptist Hill.—Four Brothers, Canal Swimmers, A. C., W. B., H. R. and C. G. Stewart.

Girl Snowballed Mules!

I worked for Miles Greenwood many years ago and loaded many a canal boat with hay, corn and other produce from his farm in Glendale. Also used to shoot muskrats and mud turtles along the bank. My wife used to throw snowballs at the towpath mules when she was a girl and she wants to be enrolled also in "the Canal Club."—Thomas E. Underwood, Florist, Newport.

Woman Scientist Joins, Too!

Dr. Norma Sauer Selbert, professor in the College of Medicine, Ohio State University, Columbus, O., and an authority in the field of public health, joins the club, writing: "I skated, played, went boating and threw sticks and stones in the canal."

I was initiated in the Race street gang by jumping off the Liberty street bridge. In doing so I hit the bottom and there I was, stuck head down in the mud, and the gang had to pull me out.—William Herbert.

DUCKS AT ST. BERNARD ENJOYED SWIMMING ON CANAL WATERS, TOO! W. H. BOONE PHOTO.

Miles Greenwood, Founder of Fire Department, One of Greatest Characters in Canal History

President of the old Cincinnati Volunteer Fire Department, organizer of the new "paid' department, a leader in the establishment of the Ohio Mechanics' Institute, proprietor for over half a century of the large iron foundry at the canal and Walnut street, Miles Greenwood was one of the greatest "canal boys" in the history of the city.

Born in Jersey City in 1807, he settled near Cincinnati with his father in 1817 and about 1832 established on the Miami Canal the Eagle Iron Works, which soon became the largest in the West, says the History of the Cincinnati Fire Department. His buildings were destroyed by fire in 1852, but were rebuilt. In 1861 Greenwood turned the foundry into an arsenal, where he employed over 700. He turned out 200 bronze cannon, the first made in the West, hundreds of caissons and gun carriages, and a seagoing monitor, and 40,000 Springfield muskets were turned into rifles. The foundry was set on fire three times during the war. Gatling invented the revolving Gatling gun in 1861 and the first of these guns were made at the Greenwood foundry during the Civil War when Walter A. Edwards, Sr., father of E. W. Edwards, president of the Rapid Transit Commission, was superintendent of that foundry.

Greenwood, a man of huge size, great physical endurance and strong determination, joined the volunteer fire department in 1829 and became its leader and president. The various volunteer companies became centers of political influence and keen rivalry developed between them. This led to many street fights among the volunteers responding to fires, and culminated in a free-for-all fight between the companies at the planing mill fire at John and Augusta streets in 1851. The volunteers fought each other all night and permitted the mill to burn down!

In 1853, against the bitter opposition of the volunteers, a paid fire department was organized, with Miles Greenwood as chief engineer. In the same year Latta constructed the first steam fire engine at Cincinnati—built in part at the Greenwood foundry. The volunteers, using hand pumps, were bitterly opposed to the steam pump. On a memorable day in 1853 the heavy steam pump, drawn by four horses, left the Greenwood foundry to go to its first fire—at Fourth and Sycamore streets. "It was well understood that the buildings had been fired by the members of the volunteer companies, who were bittedly opposed to the introduction of the steam engine, for the purpose of having an opportunity of smashing it," says the fire department history. "Greenwood was soon surrounded by 300 of these men, who were loud in their threats of vengeance. But his cool courage and resolute will daunted the rioters."

Greve says: "When the bell struck the alarm an enormous crowd gathered around the engine at Greenwood's shop. No one was willing to drive the team, and finally Greenwood himself took charge of the engine and swung out into the street, followed by his new firemen (of the paid department) in their splendid uniforms. With him came the men of his great foundry and Jacob W. Piatt, surrounded by 255 of his Irish retainers. The expected fight (between the volunteer and paid departments) came off, but lasted only a short time. Greenwood, with his bright helmet and big trumpet, was the leader in the fray, and after about thirty minutes' loss of time and the smashing of a few heads, the volunteer companies were driven off and left with no weapons but their own engines. With these they tried to show greater efficiency than their new opponents, but failed. Two other fires occurred that night and the success of the new engine was so great as to end the opposition to the paid fire department."

Miles Greenwood died in 1885. The Ohio Mechanics' Institute, that he was so largely instrumental in founding, now occupies the site of his plant, and some years previously the Banner Brewery was located there.

Picnic for Whole Village!

When the water was low in the canal we shot fish, principally carp. I remember two very interesting summer canal boat picnics, one of which was given to the village of Glendale in general by J. C. Richardson.—Dudley M. Bartlett.

Two "Cops" That Beat As One!

As a boy I often had to get out of the canal and run when the cry of "Cop!" was raised. But now I am on the police force, and have had as my police partner the "cop" who chased me out of the canal many a time as a lad.—Jacob Schardt, police sergeant.

"FIRE IN CINCINNATI!"—FROM OLD LONDON NEWSPAPER. HOW EARLY FIRES ALONG THE CANAL WERE FOUGHT.

Wintry Night Turned to Day by Great Strobridge Fire in 1887

W. H. Merten, vice president of the Strobridge Lithographing Company and president of the Cincinnati Club, who in his boyhood days was "a day and night swimmer" in the canal, recalls the great fire at the Strobridge factory, located along the towpath near Race street.

"That fire occurred in the early morning hours of December 1, 1887—the date is indelibly burned into my memory," said Mr. Merten.

"I have many happy memories of the canal—but December 1, 1887, gave me a dreadful shock. As a boy I swam in the canal hundreds of times—by day at the famous White Fence that inclosed the House of Refuge, by night at Brighton. The White Fence was our favorite daylight swimming hole, for there were no residences nearby and we could swim as we pleased without fear of being driven away.

"I had secured a position in the office of the Strobridge the year the new plant was built in 1884. When I went to work December 1, 1887, with my lunch under my arm, turned the corner at Elm and Canal streets and saw the great and beautiful new factory with its fine towers collapsed in ruins and gutted by fire, my heart sank."

But young Merten remained with the company through all the years—the plant was rebuilt and the former office boy is now vice president of the concern.

The newspaper accounts of the fire estimated the loss at from $400,000 to $500,000. The great plant burst into flames at 1 o'clock in the wintry morning. The origin was a mystery. The fire was most spectacular.

"With flames leaping high into the sky and turning night into the brightness of day, with sparks shooting everywhere in pyrotechnical display, the scene was a weirdly beautiful one, notwithstanding the fact that it cost over half a million dollars to produce it," said one account. "Huge lithographing stones came hurtling down through the floors with a roar, before towers and walls and floors collapsed, and great presses, machinery, building and vast stores of paper and lithographs for the leading theatrical productions of the time were destroyed. The plant was the largest of the kind in the world. The famous Matt Morgan war pictures, valued at $50,000, went up in smoke."

Large Fires of Early Days in Canal District

M. Werk & Co.'s soap and candle factory, on Poplar street, west of the canal, burned with a loss of $170,000 on November 6, 1874. Strobel's picture frame factory, Canal, near Elm street, was destroyed with a loss of about $40,000 on January 30, 1874. J. H. Sanning's planing mill, Fourteenth and Plum streets, around which many canal swimmers used to play, was destroyed with a loss of over $50,000 on May 12, 1874. On May 14, 1891, there was a fire and explosion at the Moerlein brewery, Elm street, just off the canal to the east, and Fireman Henry Smith fell seventy-five feet to his death from the roof. The loss was about $40,000, and in the same year there was a large fire, with explosions, that destroyed the five-story structure of the Clifton Springs distillery, one of the large industries of old days along the canal.

"Knee Deep in Spring" and "A Big Schooner!"

AT ST. MARY'S, O., OVER HALF A CENTURY AGO

John J. Hauss, who drove mules on the canal sixty years ago, and is now druggist at St. Mary's, O., has poetic ideas. He sends us this beautiful canal view, taken over half a century ago at St. Mary's, and he writes poetically about "wading knee deep in spring," and has something to say about old boats and "schooners." He writes:

> I drove canal mules sixty years ago. The canal days were the happiest of my life. I would like to live them over again and wade "knee deep in spring" on the towpath and get back to dear old Cincinnati and get one of those big, old-fashioned schooners with free lunch—over the Rhine!

Old Permit to Cut Ice

Jacob Schlachter, meat packer, sends in a copy of the license that his father obtained from the State of Ohio in 1875, giving him permission to cut ice on the canal for the winter of that year. The license says that the banks shall not be injured nor navigation obstructed by the ice cutters.

J. W. writes: In the saloon on the canal bank below the Mohawk bridge was this motto in German:

Gott segne deinen Eingang wenn du Durst hast,

Deinen Ausgang wenn du bezahlt hast.

Which means: Blessings on your entrance, if you are thirsty, and on your exit, if you have paid.

Eight Killed in Explosion at Fire on Canal

The greatest disaster that ever occurred along the canal was the fire and explosion that destroyed Pugh & Alvord's pork house at Canal and Walnut streets, with the loss of eight or nine lives, on Saturday, February 25, 1843. The flames were discovered in the smoke house, in the rear of the main building, at 5 p. m. It was thought that by closing all openings leading into the main building the blaze could be confined to the smoke house. But after half an hour the smoke and inflammable gas from the smoke house made its way through a tunnel into the main building, despite the closing of the tunnel doors. When these doors were burned through the flames ignited the gases that filled the main building. A tremendous explosion followed. The roof of the main building was blown off into the street, the walls were blown out and the whole structure collapsed. Joseph Bonsall, Caleb Taylor, H. S. Edmonds, J. S. Chamberlain, foreman of the Hook and Ladder Company, H. C. Merrill, John Ohe and two or three others were killed, and George Shillito, Mr. Alvord and many others were injured. The whole city was thrown into mourning. The canal was frozen solid at the time.

Bonner Chips In With An Eel Story

"My chum made a dive into the canal and struck a dead hog that was floating a few inches under the surface," said Charles R. Bonner. "My friend's arm went clear through the carcass of the dead creature.

"Believe it or not—I saw a lot of live eels come swimming out of the broken carcass of the hog. I know an eel when I see one. I have caught them with hook and line. A whole school of eels came out of that hog and swam away."

"Rapid Transit" Was Name of Canal Boat

Robert C. Heinzmann of the Federal Products Company said: In 1901, when I was with the Union Distillery, Carthage, we bought, at St. Mary's, O., a canal boat that had a prophetic name, "Rapid Transit!" We kept the name on her and for years this boat made about three miles an hour transporting thousands of barrels of our whisky from Carthage to Cincinnati.

For many years the colored people were baptized in the canal at a place called Guinea Hill, about a half mile south of Bruckmann's brewery. There was shouting when the preacher would immerse them under the water.—Edward Dickmeier.

Oh! Those Good Times! Food! Drink! Fun!

Sam Bayer, 5605 Abbotsford street, who used to have fifteen skiffs for hire on the canal, writes:

"I lived at the canal, near Findlay bridge, when it was a footbridge, and when it broke down in 1861 my pal ferried people across for one and two cents apiece. There was no house from ours to Liberty street. I fished when a little kid. In a half hour I would catch six to eight catfish about eight inches long. Then we used to seine and catch a skiff-full from Bank street to Findlay street. And on holidays I used to get the crowd together and go out to Second Basin, with our lunch, bat and ball, quoits and boxing gloves and beer.

First Plunge Costly!

I took my first plunge into the muddy waters of the Miami and Erie Canal in 1858, against my father's strict order, and nearly cut one toe off. Sewed on by the then famous surgeon, Dr. Thomas Wood.—W. B. Harrison.

Swam for Ice Chunks!

My reward as a boy for getting beer for the men of the iceboats was an occasional piece of ice which was thrown overboard into the water. Of course I had to swim to get it, and quick, too, because there was always competition.—C. J. Boos, 1122 Ryland avenue, Bond Hill.

OUT FOR A DELIGHTFUL EXCURSION ALONG THE CANAL IN THEIR HOME-MADE JOHNBOAT.

Favors Towpath Super-Highway From Cincinnati to Toledo

The Middletown (O.) Civic Association joins the Canal Swimmers' Society—and urges that Cincinnati's Central Parkway be linked up with a super-highway along the old canal route to Toledo. An association has been formed to promote this cause. Frank B. Pauly, president of the Middletown association, writes:

> It was "Uncle George" Sebald, patriarch of Middletown's canal zone and president of the Bureau of Commerce of this organization, who led and won the fight in the last session of the Ohio Legislature for the abandonment of the canal for water purposes so that the right of way might be used as a motor highway.
>
> Often, in the dear dead days, did "Uncle George," with his rotund figure of nearly 300 pounds, dent the placid surface of the canal.
>
> It is interesting to recall, too, that the last boat which plied this far north on the old canal stopped in front of Uncle George's office one hot July afternoon in 1912. The gallant crew labored diligently, and perhaps profanely, for two days in an effort to raise the rusty lift bridge on old Third street, but without success. That was the death knell of canal transportation through Middletown. The 1913 flood did the rest.

Naked Lads Had To Hide In Sand Box on Street

While swimming one day Officer Schweitzer ordered us into shallow water to see if we were properly attired. We refused, so he took our clothes to the York street station. We stayed in the water till supper time, then started to run home naked. We got as far as a sand box along the Crosstown car line at the bridge, just as a car came along and we jumped into the box, pulled down the lid and there we stayed until 7 o'clock, when some of the other boys came out for an evening swim. I succeeded in getting one of the boys to go to my home and get a pair of pants, and that's the way I ran home, and did get it, and how, especially when I told dad he had to go to the police station to get my clothes.

Skating at times was too tame, and to liven things up we would cut holes in the ice, blocks of about four feet square and about five inches thick, usually four or five blocks. Running across these was called playing ticklish. After the surface of these blocks was washed over three or four times they sure were slippery, and I did it once too often and felt the icy chill of the canal at ten above zero.—George F. Hilgeman, 2647 Acosta avenue.

George F. Dieterle Tells About Old Canal Swallows!

George F. Dieterle, former president of the Chamber of Commerce, said: "As a child I tried to learn to swim in the canal—holding on to the bank and kicking my legs. When my father heard of this he took me to Robert Schmidt's Floating Bath, foot of Vine street, and had me taught how to swim. Then I went into the canal with impunity. We used to catch crawfish in the canal by using a string with a piece of meat tied at the end—and we also caught mudcats. Before the sparrows were imported we had a great many swallows along the canal—but they disappeared when the sparrows came. I remember the Sunday picnics given by sandboats up the canal to Weber's Garden in Carthage."

I built a flatboat in my aunt's cellar and the boat was two inches too wide to go through the door. Then, after rebuilding it, we paid a man a dime to put a heavy coat of sticky tar on the bottom. I sailed the Atlantic Ocean during the last war and never got any more kick out of it than on the old canal.—William C. Bold, 906 Walnut street, Dayton, Ky.

ROSS AVENUE, ELMWOOD, DRAWBRIDGE, CRANKED BY MAN TO LET BOATS PASS—LOANED BY CHARLES FEHRMANN.

Col. Procter Is Club's Champion Duck Shooter

"I believe I can qualify for membership in the Old Canal Society, for when I was a boy I used to skate on the canal east of Glendale, and had many enjoyable days along the old stream. And in my early days, too, I used to shoot ducks along the canal," said Col. William Cooper Procter.

Col. Procter is the first member to make any reference to duck-shooting along the canal, and has been elected Champion Duck Shooter of the society.

Captain of Fleet of Canal Boats in Great Flood

Frank E. Stevenson, who lived here seventy years, and is now retired at Los Angeles after fifty-two years' service as railroad representative, saved a colored boy from drowning in the canal in 1870, and was captain of a fleet of canal boats carrying railroad passengers in the flood of '84. He writes: "During the great flood, when trains could not operate up the flooded Millcreek Valley, I suggested we run canal boats to a point near Winton Place and St. Bernard. My suggestion was acted on and I was made captain of a fleet of two canal boats—one for baggage and one for passengers holding tickets to points on the C., H. & D. and Atlantic & Great Western or Erie Railroad, and both lines did a large business. Many people made the trip, for 25 cents, just to get a good view of the flooded Millcreek Valley."

Mud-balled Only Boy Who Had Bathing Suit

On one occasion, in the rear of Adams's brewery, where our gang and another were in swimming, there appeared a fellow in a bathing suit! Bathing suits weren't worn often in those days by the canal swimmers. We put him in the middle of the canal, lined up on both sides and mud-balled him until he consented to take his bathing suit off. We finally left him standing in the middle of the water, crying.—William C. Knodel.

Lived in Canal State House!

From 1903 until 1912 my father was in charge of canal repairs, kept the canal in condition so the boats could run. We lived in what was known as the State House, on the canal opposite the falls at Cumminsville, and we swam at the falls, the Willows and Sandy Bottom.—Earl Blersch, Northside.

Gasoline Canal Boat "Got Stuck!"

Harry R. Stevens, Maplewood avenue, who gave some interesting canal data, writes that when he caught his first fish, a carp, in Dietz's Basin, he was so proud of it that he let all the street car passengers admire it, too! He adds:

"My father was a great lover of the beauty of the old canal and he and I took a ride from Lockland to Cincinnati on what was then the last word in canal boats. It was of similar shape to previous canal boats, but had a steel hull with wood cabin, and instead of being pulled by mules, had a gasoline engine, so installed that the propeller did not throw any waves (in compliance with the State law) so as not to wash away the banks and levees. We ran aground on a mud flat or, as the captain said, 'a bar,' where we were 'stuck' for an hour. We eventually cleared the bar by pushing 'all together' on long poles from the roof of the cabin."

Pulled Skiffs to Beer Garden!

Minus bathing suits, we would sit on the canal bank after supper, and when daylight had sufficiently passed, the cop would wave his club—"All right, boys." It took just a few seconds; off came a pair of pants and a shirt, and "Oh, boy," it was great.

All coal shipped by boat was loaded just in front of the Armleder plant.

On Sunday afternoon, our neighbors would get together with their skiffs, load them with the women and children, and each boat tied to the other, the men would take to the towpath and pull the boats to a beer garden near Brighton. Returning, each boat would be floated with the current, and with folk song we finally reached our homes on the "good old canal," which, after all, is a pleasant memory.—Charles Bertram.

OLD CITY HOSPITAL, ON CANAL AT TWELFTH STREET, WITH BOYS FISHING ON OPPOSITE SHORE.

"Oh, joy! Such happy days as I had along this canal! I always will be thankful for the old canal!" writes Marie Bender, 413 West McMicken avenue, who loaned this photograph of the old City Hospital.

The Canal Scribe was hospital reporter years ago and paid daily visits to the City Hospital. The picture brings back a flood of memories—of witnessing wonderful operations by the great surgeons of those days, of seeing the devoted scientists in the hospital laboratory and being permitted to help some of them stain their microscope slides, of seeing the various disease germs growing in culture tubes and spending instructive hours in the hospital museum and library. And of course the scribe recalls the lovely nurses.

"Because the canal flowed by the hospital the erroneous idea prevailed that there were miasmatic exhalations from the canal that caused hospital patients to have malarial fevers, and so quinine was often given the fevered patients," commented Dr. Harry H. Hines, well-known surgeon, who was interne at the hospital in 1898. "This was before the discovery of the real cause of malaria."

One day a mother rushed into the hospital carrying her baby that had accidentally swallowed carbolic acid. The babe's throat was too small to admit the stomach pump—so Dr. Walter Griess inserted a tiny tube down the throat and into the stomach and with his mouth sucked out the poison, burning his lips but saving the child! Again a child fell into the canal at the hospital. The doctors worked for hours to resuscitate it—but in vain. At the hospital every day brought its heartache and tragedy—but there lingers in memory the integrity and devotion of the hospital staff. Here the Canal Scribe years ago reported the meetings presided over by Mayor Julius Fleischmann and at which Dr. C. R. Holmes discussed his plans for the big new General Hospital on the hilltops.

R. M. Fleming, formerly of Piqua—One day I opened the canal wickets to provide shower baths for our gang.

Attorney Robert P. Hargitt—On a dare, I swam in the canal one cold day just after the ice broke up. Again, with camp equipment, I rowed six miles up the canal.

When a boatman caught us stealing a ride, he would make us pump out the water that had leaked in on the voyage. —Joseph F. Kouba.

I saw a man, driving a canal-boat mule, fall dead off the mule of heart disease. He fell into the canal.—W. A. Minten, Newport.

Nearly 500 Barrels of Whiskey Carried In Single Cargo By Whiskey Boat On Canal

Don't get excited, boys! Calm yourselves while you are being informed that in gazing upon the picture on the opposite page you are looking at over $1,000,000 (one million dollars) worth of first-class whisky!

That's the estimate at current bootleg prices—and without any "cutting" and watering!

That boat carries nearly 500 barrels—say 25,000 gallons or 100,000 quarts. At $10 a quart, that's $1,000,000—and with a little generous watering the figure jumps to two millions!

A. J. Weichold, 4047 Herron avenue, Cumminsville, gives an interesting account of his experience as whisky boat driver for the old Clifton Springs Distillery.

"We hauled cargoes of whisky, spirits and alcohol that would have made a bootlegger of today turn green with envy—if our cargoes were figured at bootleg prices.

"It was not uncommon to load a boat with a cargo of 350 to 450 barrels of whisky.

"Imagine what hijackers would do to a boat crew today if they were to attempt a trip of this kind without an army for protection.

"After leaving the distillery it was customary, when we reached the old Second Basin, behind the Workhouse, to knock a bung out and draw off a gallon or two of whatever kind of liquor we happened to have. This was done for the benefit of the canal 'roustabouts,' whom we would pick up on our way down to Music Hall, where we would unload.

"As they were, as a general rule, hard characters, we would give them a shot or two to brace them up. After landing the boat, they would commence unloading the cargo, which was placed on the bank directly behind Music Hall, from where it was hauled to its destination.

"During the unloading of the boat drinks were dealt out at regular intervals in just sufficient quantity to each man so as to permit him to keep up steam. When most of the cargo was unloaded they were given all they could drink.

"It was the duty of the 'skinner' or driver to keep down trouble by threatening with the heavy butt of his whip, which was a mean weapon in anyone's hands, especially if swung from the saddle.

"After unloading, empties were usually taken on.

"Because it was difficult to turn the boat at the Plum street elbow, we usually towed the boat, stern first, back to Second Basin.

"The time consumed was about three hours one way when five horses were used (we used no mules at the distillery) and about three and one-half hours, loaded, when two or three horses were used with a light load.

"We operated three boats—The City of Cincinnati, The Clifton Springs and The City of Toledo."

Canal Swimmer Became City's Champion Diver!

One of our well-known officials in the Fire Department was rescued by another lad and myself after he had gone down twice.

Another one of our crowd from Walnut Hills was William Dardis, who afterward became lifesaver at Chester Park and a fancy diver, and was for a long while champion diver of Cincinnati.—John F. Mitchell.

Fire Department Ran Into Canal!

Dr. Carl Hiller will also recall that when the roof of the house we were living in at Madison and Elm took fire the Fire Department, thinking they were on Fifteenth street, ran smack into the canal and the other firemen had to lay off the job until the "injine" and hose reel were dragged from the canal. Our fathers put out the fire.

Those were the happy days!—A. Theo. Schulte, Newport, Ky.

THE "WHISKY BOAT" MADE REGULAR TRIPS INTO CINCINNATI FROM DISTILLERY AT CARTHAGE—PHOTO LOANED BY FELIX KOCH.

"How We Fooled the Cop!"

The canal falls was the scene of Saturday night bathing for young and old. How many remember old Indian Joe? He taught us many tricks. He would get us boys to gather vegetables from our fathers' gardens and would catch a chicken and cook a stew in a large kettle.

Our bathing spot on the canal was at the Clapper Hill. Many a day we put a fast one over on the cops. We would hang old clothes on the fence and take our good clothes and hide them in the woods!—Herman McFarland.

W. H. Schrader, 1701 Chase Street—I swam in the canal away back in the fifties—and the "cops" chased us even in those early days!

"Mohawker" Writes—It was the 8 o'clock bell at Hauck's Brewery that was the signal for all the boys to jump in at night.

With Baby in Buggy Searched for Chum!

My chum did not have as much fun as the rest of us, because he always had one or two babies to take care of. One day I told him I'd take care of the kid brother so he could take a swim. His clothes were in the baby carriage, and the cops came. I walked away with the baby screaming for dear life. Then began the hunt for my chum, so I could get rid of baby and clothes. I did not find him till nearly noon.—Ed McCullough, Norwood.

L. W. Radina, 865 Academy avenue, thinks he has a record—caught thirty-five sunfish, big as his hand, in one hour in the canal!

"I took the grand leap into the canal from the top of the rail at the Fifteenth street bridge—and got a dollar as the grand prize," writes Harry Letch.

Hurrah! Girl Saved Lives of Two Boys And Received a Reward of Ten Dollars!

I was often whipped for swimming in the canal, but the only time I escaped a thrashing was when I saved the lives of two boys, named Winkler. They were neighbors of ours. I didn't get a medal for my bravery, but instead it was a check for $10 from Mr. Winkler. Many times I rode with Frank Lawrence and John Kinzel, the boatman with a wooden leg. They were boat owners.—Louise Flaig (nee Ranninger), 2700 Jefferson avenue

Blind Horses Fell In! Let's Help Pull 'Em Out!

Most rag men, delivering ink on the canal near Vine street, seemed to have blind horses. While waiting, the horses would wander too near the canal bank, and in would go horse and wagon. One of the workmen employed by Pete De Roo or Barney Meyer, broom factories, would caw three times like a crow, heard from Race to Sycamore—the signal something was doing. Bridges would be lined with people watching operations of rescue. The horses would be unhitched and were pulled out with ropes—and the wagons, too.—William E. Strohfeldt.

Playing "Conqueror" Was Fun!

Mr. Chairman of the Old Time Canal Sports: Did you ever play "Conqueror" on the old canal when the ice broke up? Follow the leader! It was dangerous fun; hopping and running from one large cake over several small ones to a place of safety. We always had a large fire on the bank, so those that fell in could dry before going home.—J. F. Cullman, 1918 Horton street.

"Beer Kegs!"

F. Krippe sent in a picture entitled "Beer Kegs," showing many kegs made by the John Megley Cooperage Company, Mohawk. "The bunch of good canal boys seen in the picture," he writes, "are Ben Binkert, John Zimmerman, Dr. Cantzler, Adam Schwalbach, 'Red' Kruetz, Martin Schmerr and Romey Schabertier."

Oh, the Beautiful Lanes in Clifton That Led to Canal!

"I wish to thank you for the articles in the Times-Star about the old canal, for they bring back vividly to my mind the dear scenes of my childhood," writes the Rev. C. A. Daniel, former Cincinnatian, brother of Mrs. Louis Hartmann, Sycamore street, and now a pastor in Chicago.

"As a boy I went swimming near Walnut street, laying my clothes on the flasks of the Greenwood foundry. Here I was nearly drowned, had not a larger boy pulled me out by the hair. On another occasion, while swimming, I swallowed some water and got the cholera. We lived on Mulberry street at the time. During the vacation days we would walk up to Mt. Auburn, through Corryville, then through Clifton. Oh, how well I remember those beautiful lanes, palatial residences, pretty gardens, the woods full of walnut, butternut, beech, hickorynut trees. I still remember the lanes here to the right, there to the left, until we reached the place where we crossed through the woods and the cow pastures to the canal and the place for our afternoon swim near Erkenbrecher's starch factory. The tallest boy would wade across, carrying our clothes high over his head to the towpath on the other side. Then we would follow another pathway homeward."

"Soaps" Was Rendezvous

We played at "Soaps," located midway between Mohawk and Baymiller street bridges. The lot was formerly occupied by a soap factory. Every morning we waited for the daily packet boat, Videtta, to come down from the Clifton Springs distillery.—Louis A. Sauer.

Canal Tomboy Happy Grandmother Now!

MRS. JUNG AND GRANDDAUGHTER, JEAN SKIRVIN.

Who's that pretty boy with auburn locks playing on the canal?

How he can dive and swim and jump the boats and row!

But that's not a boy!

That's a jolly girl—"Red Head Stella!"—in her brother's clothes—the happiest tomboy that ever played on the canal.

"Red" was in her glory on the towpath thirty-five and forty years ago—all Cumminsville hailed her as the girl who excelled in boyish games.

A happy, innocent lass, as full of merry pranks as the hoydenish heroine in "O Lady of Quality." But her red hair has turned gray, she is a successful wife and mother now, approaching fifty, has had nine children and is a grandmother.

She is also winner of grandmother beauty prizes, dancing and cooking prizes.

She is Mrs. Estella Meyer Jung, 1713 Sutter avenue, wife of Gottlob Jung, noted canal swimmer and member of the Gilmore Boat Club, famous for its festive parties.

"Our home was right on the canal when I was a girl and I played on the canal with my brothers for years, swam, rowed, fished, jumped on boats from bridges—everybody called me 'Red' and 'Tomboy,'" Mrs. Jung said. "Wearing my dress, I went in swimming every day. Father had two skiffs and Saturday nights would take us out with a grind organ, guitar and mouth harmonica—and a keg of beer and lunch. At thirteen I was rowing a boat when it became stuck, and in trying to pry it loose with the oar I upset it and we all fell in the canal. As a prank I sometimes wore brother William's clothes, and he wore mine. I saw a carriage go into the canal at Elm street—horses and all the pallbearers were wet up to their necks. At Second Basin a wild bull chased a little colored boy into the water. The boy was drowned and I saw them searching for his body.

"On the Fourth of July I paraded with the other girls on the canal bank in our red-white-and-blue tissue paper dresses. On New Year's Eve. we would fill wash boilers with rocks and make a noise with them. We made a camp on the canal of weeds and boards. In winter we made fires on the ice and fried things in a tin-can. We also had an Indian pot—on three sticks. I cooked wieners, too.

"One day we broke mother's skillet. We put the wet fish in the hot iron skillet which exploded and we thought some one shot us. We used to drop from bridges onto passing sandboats, and they called us the daredevils!

"But it was all great fun!"

Captain Walsh Tells of Boats Buried in Carthage

I had many experiences on the old canal, my father being an owner of a line of boats for many years. The names of some of his boats were the Oliver Perin, H. H. Lippelmann, Marietta, Celtic, Sidney, Fashion, Neptune, Sand King and Wave.

These boats were used in shipping lumber, corn, whisky, coal, and later sand and gravel used in the construction of some of our early built skyscrapers and for the paving of most of the streets of Cincinnati at that time.

I have done all kinds of work on the canal, acting as captain, bowsman, driver, loading and unloading merchandise, and sometimes helped with picnics on the sand boats on a moonlight ride. The sand boats were about the last boats on the canal. Some of them are buried in an ice pond near Carthage.—W. R. Walsh.

Canal Bridge Collapsed!

One morning as a schoolmate and I were going to school, we had come over the old Fourteenth street bridge and got about half way between Plum and Elm streets, when the bridge sank into the canal and disappeared, so we had a narrow escape. On another occasion there was a fire in one of the factories along Plum street, near Wade, and one of the engines fell into the canal.—Fred A. Willet, 3127 Eden avenue.

Packer Had Unique Paddle Wheel Pleasure Boat

Over half a century ago, when I was nine years old, I was thrown into the canal at Greenwood's foundry. We boys dove off the foot bridge at Bank street until one lad's head was cut open on a piece of crockery. Two butchers fought a terrible battle with their butcher knives on this bridge many years ago. The pork packer, Benninger, invented a canal pleasure boat with paddle wheels like the side wheels of river steamers. Nightly he would take his family out in the boat. It was a common thing in the old days to see a skiff in every back yard in Brighton for the boys and girls who enjoyed the canal.—Gustav R. Werner.

"Bronze Tablet on Parkway Should Tell Story of Canal!"

Cris Mottern, St. Bernard, who sent in a number of pretty canal scenes, makes the interesting and worthwhile suggestion that two tablets be placed at Vine street and the Parkway telling about the old canal and "Over-the-Rhine." Mottern, who was formerly a canal boatman in the East and later enjoyed fishing in the Miami and Erie Canal, writes:

"I was one of the first through the Times-Star to recommend that the Parkway be called 'The Towpath.'

"I would also suggest that a bronze tablet be placed on opposite corners at Parkway and Vine with an inscription telling of the canal, and why after crossing the bridge they called it 'Over the Rhine.'" He tells the following canal story:

"One foggy morning the captain gave the driver a lantern to carry on the towpath so he could see to steer by. Everything was going along nicely when the driver happened to think that there was a watermelon patch over some distance from the towpath. Instead of him setting the lantern down he carried it with him. The captain naturally thought there was a big bend in the canal and steered his two boats that way, when he found himself running the boats up on the towpath! The language that was used by that captain would have raised a stuffed buffalo's hair!"

Happy Times in Canal!

Thousands have taken a swim in the canal in the vicinity of the old Frietsch & Zeidler pork packing house, on the canal bank at Plum and Magnolia streets—above Fourteenth—and shown in some of your pictures. That building, with its cellars and meat hooks, still stands. My father, brother, uncle Sigmund Frietsch and myself all had happy times on the canal.—Carl Frietsch.

Girls Saved by Canal Boat!

Happy canal days! When I was 17 years old three of us girls were hunting flowers. A farmer's dog came and frightened us. We fled and climbed over a barbed wire fence, tearing our Sunday clothes! But a canal boat appeared on the scene and carried us to safety.—Marie Bender.

CANOEING ON CANAL—PHOTO FROM W. P. McCRONE.

Pursued by "Cop;" Fled Into Ice Box!

I was swimming in the old canal in 1880, when Officer Siepl chased me, with my garments in my hat, down Elder street to the Market House. There I ran into the ice box of one of the butcher shops—and dressed in the ice box! My pals were John Knagg, Joe More and John Landfried.—John Koch, Norwood.

Private Bridge Over Canal

My father, Walter Dixon, built a row of ten houses fronting on the canal opposite Queen City avenue many years ago, but the only way to get to them was to swim across or via rowboat, so it became necessary to build a bridge, which he did, probably the only privately owned bridge across the canal in Cincinnati. I attended the first "do away with the canal" meeting at the ol Central Turner Hall about thirty-seven years ago.—Walter S. Dixon.

William I. Hart, Gilbert Avenue—Jumping off boats from one to another while going in the opposite direction.

Henry Delfindahl, Slack Street—Eighty years ago I swam across the canal under the Sycamore bridge.

Lad Was Thrown In!

At seven years old I had my first swim. I was walking along the canal when an unknown man came along and pitched me out into the water, never looked back, hastening on. I ran home to Linn street and I never let a word be known.—A. Spitzmiller, New Richmond, O.

How Ludeke Was Saved

"With my older brother, Carl, and a younger brother, Robert, I was walking along the canal bank between Walnut and Main streets, when Carl and I looked around and saw Robert, six years old, struggling in the water," writes Richard B. Ludeke, Stratford avenue. "Carl jumped in and tried to catch him and then I jumped in, but it was too deep for us. A fireman from the Banner Brewery came to the rescue. Bob was rolled on a barrel until they got the water out of him, and then all three of us were sent home in a laundry wagon. If it hadn't been for that fireman there probably would not be a Robert A. Ludeke, attorney, alive here today."

Michael Devito, Hutchins Avenue—One day while I was swimming in the canal a crab got hold of my toe. It was a long time before I ventured into the canal again.

Chief Justice Wm. H. Taft, Former President of United States, Swam and Fished in the Old Canal

Now comes this welcome letter from a boyhood playmate of William H. Taft, with the interesting news that the Chief Justice of the Supreme Court and former President of the United States was also a Canal Swimmer:

CHIEF JUSTICE WM. H. TAFT

Mr. Charles Ludwig:

Many fishing trips did W. H. Taft and myself, with his brother Harry, make to Brown's Basin and the canal in Clifton.

Harry was always the custodian of the lunch basket which Mrs. Taft put up for us, and as Will was hard to get out of bed in the morning, we arranged to tie a string with a stone at one end and the other to Bill's big toe. At 4 o'clock I arrived at Bill's house and no string, so I concluded that he had overlooked it. I then tossed a few pebbles into the open window and shortly I saw Bill's smiling face and heard a "Ho, ho, ha!" He said that he had been dreaming and had wound the string around his leg.

We arrived at the basin fishing in the morning, and in the afternoon, meeting some other boys, we went swimming in the canal. A canal boat came gliding along with the pilot wearing a high coachman's hat with a brass button on the side. One of the boys reached down and, grasping a handful of clay, threw it into the air, and when it came down it landed squarely on the top of that red-headed pilot's hat. He grabbed for it, it toppled and fell into the canal and sank out of sight. He swung the boat into the bank and, as Bill Taft was laughing hard, the pilot caught him and was going to chastise him, but the boy who threw the mud dove into the canal and came up on the other bank, so the red-headed pilot dropped Bill and, grabbing a half brick, threw it with an oath, saying that he was marked for life.

I think this entitled W. H. Taft to a place in the Canal Club, as "Lub" and myself are the only two that are left of the old canal crowd that used to guard Southern and Auburn avenues with snowballs.

Yours, OLD MT. AUBURN, 1873.

Mr. Taft is welcomed into the Canal Swimmers' Society with highest honors, with his old playmate of '73. The society feels proud that it has given the Nation a President and Chief Justice. A copy of the above letter was forwarded to the Chief Justice and his happy reply appears on the next page.

Yes, the Chief Justice was an ardent canal swimmer in his boyhood. He was so enthusiastic about it that he would "stay all day" and was so badly sunburned that he had to have a doctor and go to bed. And with a merry twinkle in his eye the Chief Justice says that he is quite sure the freckles caused by that dose of sunburn can still be found on his back!

> **Chief Justice Taft Tells How He Was Badly Sunburned Swimming All Day at Brown's Basin**

Supreme Court of the United States
Washington, D.C.

February 16, 1929.

My dear Mr. Ludwig:

I thank you for sending me your articles on the old Canal. I never recollect having gone into the old Canal before or after it reached Brown's basin and Mummert's basin. Our crowd from Mount Auburn very much enjoyed swimming in Brown's basin. So far did we carry it that we would stay there all day. I remember one occasion of this kind when the sun was very hot and we were there all day and were so much exposed that the next day my back was so burned that I had to have a doctor and remain in bed. I had planned to join an excursion to Mammoth Cave in a party, but I had to give up the party and wait for some little time until the skin peeled off. I am quite sure that an examination of my back will still show the freckles that were the result of that day's excursion.

Sincerely yours,

Wm H Taft

Brown's Basin, the favorite swimming hole of Chief Justice Taft in his boyhood days, was also known as Blair's, Dietz's and Hinsch's Basin, so Elmer E. Humphries of the Rapid Transit Commission, an authority on canal geography, explains. It was the largest of the group of basins formed by the waters of the canal in the Clifton vicinity, and was located on the towpath just above Clifton avenue. Mummert's Basin, also mentioned by the Chief Justice, was near by. Both are shown on the map on page 19.

Take a Ride on Steam Launch— The Cost Is Only Five Cents!

Jacob Hoffmann, 2943 Urwiler avenue, Westwood, who lived near the canal for over half a century around Brighton, was so enthusiastic about our canal yarns in the Times-Star that he prepared eight scrap-books of these stories and sent them to eight members of the old Schoolmates Association now living in various parts of the country from New York to Portland, Ore. Hoffmann played along the canal from Civil War days on. He writes:

"An old song of those days was:

>   Mother, may I go out to swim?
>   Yes, my darling daughter;
>   Hang your clothes on a hickory limb,
>   But don't you go near the water.

"As a small boy, I fled from the policemen who found us swimming—we carried our clothes across the canal to escape and dressed in Browne's apple orchard. There we hung our clothes on an apple tree—not a hickory limb—to dry.

"The canal, especially in the less public spots, swarmed with boys and ofttimes men during the summer months. The boys of our neighborhood usually took to the canal in the rear of Forbus's or Eckert's tanneries, Reynolds's ice house, Maas's furniture store or Enyart's grocery, between Mohawk bridge and the Brighton House. Beyond these limits we felt we were in the Mohawk or the Goosetown territory. As boys we used to like to go up to the canal bank and sit on the drays, of which there were always several in the rear of the tanneries. (For the benefit of young folks of today who, perhaps, never saw a dray and do not know what one looked like, it may be added there is a good picture of a dray on the left side of Foote's canal painting, reproduced on page 15 of this book.)

"Skiffs were numerous on the canal in our boyhood days. Especially did those boys whose homes abutted on the stream seek to be owner or part owner of a skiff. At one time during several summer seasons a steam-propelled boat, somewhat larger than the ordinary skiff, plied the waters of the old canal from a point below Mohawk bridge to far beyond Brighton and Cumminsville. It was owned and operated by Frank Lorenz, and the charge for a ride on it was five or ten cents per trip, according to the distance traveled. Many will remember the shrill steam whistle on the launch, announcing its arrival at the various stopping places. The owners of skiffs all were bent on selecting a favorite name to paint thereon. Among them were such as the Dolly Varden, Mohawk Indian, Brighton Star, Champion, Excelsior, Butcherboy, etc. Picnic parties on the canal were numerous, and at the head of Baymiller street large crowds gathered awaiting the departure of the canal boats for Ludlow Grove and other picnic places."

Here's a jolly crowd of little boys swimming in the canal in the basin at Clifton. The picture was taken years ago and we wonder if the happy face of a Chief Justice and former President is among them—for William Howard Taft swam there. The picture was loaned by J. R. Pigman.

BEAUTIFUL BROWN'S BASIN, CLIFTON, WHERE CHIEF JUSTICE TAFT SWAM AS A BOY—PHOTO FROM W. H. BOONE

Seventeen Jolly Printers Laid Off for a Day, Gayly Rowed Flotilla Out the Towpath Way!

Why work when a bright and joyous summer day beckons you to enjoy a merry skiff ride in the free outdoors along the old canal?

This happy thought entered the minds of seventeen union printers simultaneously many years ago—and they quit for the day and took the outing. Philip Pfalzgraf, our veteran composing room superintendent, was one of the seventeen.

They put substitute printers on their jobs, rented three skiffs, obtained three tin buckets, and started on a carefree expedition up the canal.

"We started downtown, rowed out to Mohawk and Brighton and proceeded to a genial taproom for a little rest and refreshment," Phil reminisced. "When our memorable voyage began the oarsmen of the Printers' Flotilla distinguished themselves by their pretty and skilful seamanship. Passers-by along the canal commented on the dainty 'feather-edged' rowing, the oars skimming lightly as a feather along the top of the water on the back stroke.

"From time to time we sent foraging parties to shore and they came back with plenty of lunch. I might add that those three tin buckets were not used for bailing out the skiffs. We made the canal ring with the good old popular songs of the day— seventeen printers can produce some wonderful harmony under the inspiring influence of a sunshiny holiday and the fascinating woodland scenery that graced the canal out in the suburbs. We proceeded beyond the Workhouse toward Clifton, where trees lined the banks and where the lovely open country was a glorious sight. Then came the journey back home, and though our rowing was not quite as classy as at the start we reached port safely. Some of our crew were a bit seasick from the towering canal waves, but next day seventeen printers were back on the job with refreshed and renewed spirits."

AND HE MADE THE CANOE HIMSELF OUT OF STUFF SALVAGED FROM DUMP!

Hugh R. Thompson of 502 Lombardy street, Elmwood, loaned this picture. It was taken in August, 1914, when the World War Broke out—but this happy canoeist couldn't let anything like a World War bother him or interfere with his canal joys. For he had a homemade canoe and it had to be tested out. It was made of old barrel hoops, covered with tar-paper.

"All of the material out of which the canoe was made was salvaged from a dump!" writes Thompson.

NEAR AQUEDUCT, CARTHAGE—PHOTO WILLIAM HUBER.

Here's a happy group taking a spin on the old canal in a trim and speedy power boat. The picture was taken near the aqueduct at Carthage and las loaned by William Huber, 116 West Seventieth street.

Preferred Old Canal to Modern Swimming Pool

Despite the modern playgrounds and swimming pools the kids have today, if I'd be a boy again, give me the old canal and its banks for a swimming hole and playground.—Harry G. Wolf, Bailiff, Court of Common Pleas.

I can remember one time when water ran uphill! This was the time when the old aqueduct caved in on Mitchell avenue!—Edward Hauschildt.

My husband, George Vogel, was a member of the Peerless Athletic Club, Plum, near Fifteenth, and went skiff riding about thirty-five years ago with me on the canal. My father, John Espenleiter, and son, John, Jr., worked on the canal breaking ice and drawing it into the ice storage cellar with old-fashioned ice hooks.—Mrs. Susan Vogel.

Charter Member from North! Arrested—Trial "Pleasant!"

Though I now live in Minneapolis, I feel as though I should be made a charter member of the club, as I was arrested for swimming in the canal a la natural. The arrest was made while the writer was in swimming at the turn bridge which was in the center of the canal in front of the Armleder factory and, believe me, the swimming was fine, when the officer made his appearance on the scene. Our trial was held before the eminent and beloved Juvenile Court Judge Caldwell, and I still hold the court scene in mind, for his honor made it a pleasant one.—S. C. Pollak.

I used to fish at the Lion Brewery, where there was a ten-inch pipe of hot water running late in the fall of the year and fish were plentiful around there at that time. I received the title of fisherman.—Harry J. Ell.

Help! Canal Scribe Dove and Lost His Glasses! Needed Them to See Microscopic Canal Wonders!

A flood of memories of boyhood tragedies and triumphs along the canal came into the mind of the Canal Scribe when he received this letter from a fellow swimmer of the old canal days:

> Dear Charlie Ludwig:
>
> Do you recall when you lost your gold-rimmed glasses while swimming in the canal, and how the "McMicken Gang" helped dive for them, but failed to recover them, and how you felt when you went home without them?
> GEORGE G. BAETZ.

Yes, I recall the tragedy of those lost gold-rimmed glasses. It was in the middle '90s, on a hot night, that our McMicken crowd strolled over to the canal for a swim to "cool off."

I used to swim with my glasses on. It was a magnificent dive I made off the bank into the canal that night—but the triumph quickly turned to tragedy! I came up minus the glasses! They had been washed off, for the first time, and were lost! This was a catastrophe—the glasses cost about $8—a fortune in those days. The whole McMicken crowd of swimmers aided me in the search for the glasses. The mud was two feet thick at the bottom of the canal and we tramped around in the mud and put our hands into it and rolled at the bottom and dove in vain, trying to find those glasses.

After hours of work we gave up the search near midnight and I made my way home broken-hearted and bankrupt. The glasses were my most precious possession—I could see little without them. Ruskin once said that of all the inventions only glasses had really been a boon to mankind. I felt the force of his argument then.

I was unable to finance another pair and was in despair when I went to work next morning—I was office boy at the Times-Star. But the kindly editor, Mr. George Mortimer Roe, who had befriended me in many ways and given me books to attend night school, promptly turned my sorrow to joy by getting me a new pair and stating I should pay him back for them at the rate of 25 or 50 cents a week. A few months later, when I had repaid him six of the eight dollars the glasses cost, Mr. Roe said: "Now, Charlie, you have paid faithfully each week, and I will make you a gift of the other two dollars!"

As a very small boy I practiced swimming at Second Basin, and when I mastered the art took the crowd to the canal near Findlay street to show them I could swim clear across! That was a greater triumph then than swimming across the Ohio River later.

One day, despite mother's instruction not to skate on the rather thin ice—"You'll break through," she warned—I went anyway and skated gloriously from Walnut to Vine street. I had the whole canal to myself. Not another soul ventured out on that thin ice. But as I reached the Vine street bridge the ice broke and I sank to my neck in the frigid water, and without touching bottom. The thin ice broke as I tried to crawl out on it, but I finally got out, skated back to Walnut street, took off the skates and ran all the way home to keep warm. To prevent mother from discovering

"GEM CITY" ON PLUM STREET, CALM AND UNHURRIED—WILMES PHOTO

that her prediction had come true, I went down into the cellar and put on some dry clothes that brother Bill brought me. But mother read my mind. As soon as I entered the room she said: "You fell through the ice, didn't you?"

Our crowd included Jacob Klein, Eddie Kuehn, Joe Diller, Robert Meyer, Ernst Wuerth, William Etter, Joseph Heintzman, Henry, George and William Baetz, Carl Propheter, Carl Krueger, George Eckert, William Scheidt, Charlie Goosmann, Charlie Mauthe, Charlie Baumgartner, John Koch, Lou Bauman and many others. My family contributed a quintet of towpath playmates—Adolph, Fred, William, Edward and Charles Ludwig.

Our leader was the beloved Dr. Herbert C. Shaw, who took us on many trips into the country and helped us form the McMicken football and baseball teams. We immortalized him by forming the Herbert C. Shaw Literary Forum and Symposium!

One of our canal boys, Dr. Charles Goosmann, then a young medical student, was a powerful swimmer, but found a double use for canal water. He would take home samples of the water and with his microscope show us the amazing life in it—the tiny ameba, protozoan form of life consisting of but a single cell; the daphnia, big as a pinhead, with a heart that you could see beating under the microscope, the miniature cypris clam, certain bacteria, the tiny paramecium, a slipper animalcule looking like a shoe, and the strange vorticella, with small hairs whirling like a water wheel —microscopic wonders of the canal, numbering billions, but that few of the Canal Swimmers ever saw! And in the tail of a canal tadpole he would show us the blood cells circulating! He told us about Prof. Hugo Mullert, one of the world's greatest authorities on goldfish, who raised goldfish near the canal falls. Goosmann caught and studied small snakes on the canal, and broke down the foolish fear of harmless, non-poisonous

When Powel Crosley, Jr., Made Memorable Canoe Trip on Canal and Slept on the Towpath

A month's canoe journey and vacation on the canal and adjacent streams at a total cost of $1.85!

Powel Crosley, Jr., president of the Crosley Radio Corporation, achieved that record.

"Ah, those happy canal days!" he exclaimed as he recalled his canal experiences. "Years ago four of us boys made a memorable canoe trip. We put our two canoes in the canal above the locks at Lockland and paddled and pulled them up to Dayton, then journeyed on the Mad River and shot down the Big Miami River in our canoes on a freshet and completed our month's vacation at Venice—the total expenses for each of us being $1.85!

"My brother Lewis and I and our chief engineer, Charles Kilgour, and his brother composed our party of adventuring playmates. We found that it was easier to pull the canoe up the canal with ropes than to paddle against the stream. I shall never forget how a great burst of steam came out of a huge pipe in the canal and sent a wave of water into Kilgour's canoe that nearly swamped it. One of our treasures was an acetylene lamp that fell into the canal. We searched the canal bed for it and finally I clutched it between my feet and brought it thus to the surface while my friends lifted me out of the water and onto a bridge. We had to be acrobats to climb with our canoe out of some of the steep-walled canal lock approaches. I shall never forget the night that we camped out on the canal bank and slept on the towpath, under a bridge—for there was no other place for us to go, as railroads, trolleys and highways lined both sides of the canal."

Mr. Crosley, who now employs 3,000 in one of Cincinnati's greatest industries, looked wistfully out of his office window on Colerain avenue—for only a block away was dried-up Second Basin and the path of the old canal, now a concrete ribbon, the new boulevard.

snakes. He caught snake-feeders and proved that they did not feed snakes or vice versa. Here was a new and interesting use for canal water—a scientific use. And in this connection it may be noted that Charles Dury, Cincinnati's noted entomologist, creator of the museum in the Cuvier Press Club, also caught beetles and other creatures in the canal and these now form part of his great collection of over 100,000 insects.

It may be interesting for other canal crowds that have disbanded forever to know that our McMicken crowd holds a reunion annually, and has done so for over twenty years.

Frozen Aqueduct, Mass of Ice, Was Beautiful Scene

One of the most beautiful scenes along the old towpath was the winter scene of the old frozen aqueduct which crossed Millcreek at Carthage—frozen from top to bottom. Where the water had been overflowing icicles more than six feet in diameter formed. Many times I swam at this place and would go down below and get a shower bath from the overflow. This was the only swimming hole along the canal that had a shower with it!—W. J. Newton.

She Was a Canoeist!

When the canal ice was covered with snow we would clean it off with snow scrapers and brooms so we could skate. Our greatest fun was to get a crowd together and skate from the canal bridge in St. Barnard to the workhouse and back. I shall never forget those days as long as I live! I used to row a canoe on the old canal and steer a launch owned by Charles Bitters of St. Bernard.—Alma Eslinger.

George C. Hammann, 917 Dayton Street—My great fun was swimming by day and at night catching enough minnows to supply all fishermen in town with bait.

UNDER FULL SAIL ON THE RAGING CANAL!

C. P. Stamm of the Clifton Canoe Club loaned this photograph and added this elucidation: "Here's an action picture showing members of the Clifton Canoe Club out on the raging, roaring, rarin', tearin' canal speeding in their canoe with full sail and a stiff breeze blowing. Archie Droste is at the helm, with 'Sack' Matre acting as ballast."

Canal Boat Explosion!

"I think I was on the only canal boat that ever exploded," said Joseph Dressman, 67, 3914 Tracy avenue, Covington, who was a canal boat pilot in his youth and is now manager of the Park Hills Riding School. "I was on the Silver Moon when there was a gasoline explosion on her many years ago. There was a canal boat named Orphan. A German immigrant tried to refer to her, but could not think of the name and said: 'I mean dot boat vat has no mudder and no fader.'"

A. J. Wolsifer, 546 West Liberty Street—I belonged to the famous Sling Shot County crowd. We would race miles to the canal—and the last one in was "elected."

His Father Ran One of First Canal Boats!

My father, J. T. Jones, had a contract for digging part of canal near this city. He also ran a packet line to Toledo, making splendid time, with relays of mules at various points; he also ran the first canal boat, named Ariel.—J. Franklin Jones, 520 Union Central Building.

A. V. Fuhrman, 305 Bell Block—In 1861 or '62 I was held by police for an hour for swimming in canal—though I had knickerbockers on.

Elmer Schulte, College Hill—Father caught us in the canal and was going to whip us, but when he saw how good we could swim, changed his mind.

"Many Camp Washington Girls Rode In My Skiff!" How Canal Sand Boat Sank When It Struck Log.

Theo. Keener, 4136 Jerome avenue, who gave many Camp Washington girls rides in his skiff Americus, here for the first time explains the mystery that attended the sinking of a canal boat many years ago.

"At the age of six the boys around the old Central Turner Hall on Walnut street went swimming nightly under the old bridge on Vine or Race street," he writes. "On one occasion, when the 'cops' chased us, we scrambled out, grabbed what clothes we could reach, and ran for dear life, dressed mostly in nature's garb. The next day my mother wanted to know who had given me the new underwear! Can not remember just how I argued out of this, but am sure that good mother of mine had a fair idea just where I had been. A few years later we moved to Camp Washington. One Christmas morning we skated on thin ice. I broke through and had an icy bath in about four feet of water, and I spent the rest of that Christmas Day watching the skaters from our window, until my one suit was dry enough to wear again.

"For seven years I was the proud owner of a skiff called Americus. Many Camp Washington girls had a ride in that old boat.

"Five or more of the boys would club together for an outing out in back of the old Workhouse, which we called 'Easy Grove.' On the way out we could stop at Adams's Brewery and get an eighth of good old lager for seventy-five cents, providing we returned the empty eighth. But, of course, that was back in the good old days.

"There were quite a number of harmless water snakes along the banks of the canal, and it was great sport for me to stun a half dozen with an oar and lift them into the boat, and as the hot sun would warm them, they became quite playful and would wriggle up and down the skiff.

"One morning in early April my mother called my attention to the canal. It was fairly alive with fish, mostly carp, and some of them fully four feet long. The boys fished with clubs and seines that day, and made several big catches.

"There was a big stump in the rear of our home that we decided to remove. We attached the chain of a skiff to this log, intending to tow it out to the center of the canal, expecting it to float downstream. Being thoroughly water soaked, it sank suddenly, and almost swamped the boat. A half hour later a canal boat load of sand on the way to the city hit an obstruction that sank the boat, sand and all. The canal was blocked for three days, until they could transfer what sand they could save to another boat. Of course they had to find out what really caused the accident, and brought up our old stump. There was plenty of yelling and cursing going on during this operation. To this day I do not think that anyone recognized our old log, which laid in full view for many years, and my father cautioned me never to tell a word of this."

Here's Cantaloupe King!

Stephen Gerrard, Cincinnati, America's "cantaloupe king," has crashed the gates of our club.

"Forty-four years ago I hauled merchandise from Sixth street up to the canal for shipment," he said. "I received three cents for hauling a barrel of goods, five cents for a sack and two cents for a bushel."

Edward J. Murphy, Sr., Clark Street—Sixty years ago dove into canal and came to the surface with an oyster can attached to my nose.

Spent Happy Honeymoon Skiff Riding on Canal!

My wife and I can qualify as members of the Canal Society, for, when we were married, years ago, we were unable to take an ocean voyage, so we spent our honeymoon on the canal taking delightful skiff rides. I have pictures showing our honeymoon rides on the canal. Now we live 1,200 miles away, in Florida, but we still think of the dear old days on the canal.—Mr. and Mrs. William L. Curnayn, Haines City, Fla.

Pleasure Boats In Second Basin At Workhouse Wall Where Thousands Swam.

WORKHOUSE WALL, SECOND BASIN, FLOWER COVERED—ED HEMPELMAN AT HELM OF HIS SPEEDBOAT, GRACIE H.

Thousands of Canal Swimmers who "went in" at Second Basin will recall the Workhouse wall on the other side of the basin. This picture was loaned by Edward Hempelman, 2408 Central Parkway. His father, Fred Hempelman, was a pioneer resident along the canal, opposite Queen City avenue. The Hempelmans were noted builders of canal skiffs, canoes and gasoline and steam launches. "We had thirty skiffs and canoes, and our power boats, the Gracie H, Edna and Eleanora, were known up and down the stream for the many picnic parties they carried," said Edward.

The old Hempelman home and their boathouse, where thousands rented skiffs in years gone by, was one of the most picturesque places on the canal. It was one of the few places in the city—the only one the Canal Scribe knows of—at which large trees sprang directly out of the berm-bank, that is, the bank opposite the towpath, and leaped from the water's edge high in the air and almost across the stream, forming a bower of foliage over the canal.

The picture was so charming that E. T. Hurley made an etching of it, and other artists, too, painted the scene.

Mrs. Edward Hempelman enjoyed many canal excursions with her husband. "One day we had a party at the canal falls and our friends said they would never eat carp caught in the canal," she reminisced. "But I provided a lunch of delicious pickled carp that we had caught previously in the canal, and they ate it all, two gallons, and cried for more! Then we told them they were canal carp!"

Ferd Bader, former superintendent of the workhouse, told of a frustrated effort to escape made by two prisoners working outside the wall shown above.

"Of twenty prisoners working there, two made a break to escape, but the watchful guard, Harry J. Haverkamp, now a member of Fire Company No. 6, shot twice and brought both men down. None of the eighteen tried to run when they saw that. One of the wounded men, who was colored, was struck in the neck by a single pellet from the shotgun and died."

Union Boys in '63 Drove "Johnny Reb" Away! He Came to Plum St. Bend—Prof. Lloyd Today!

Prof. John Uri Lloyd, aged 80, distinguished chemist and author, joins the Canal Swimmers' Society as its only "Johnny Reb."

His place of play and of business for sixty-five years has been right along the old canal site, a few feet from the Plum street bend, shown on the opposite page.

"I'll be happy to join the society if I can get in as a 'Johnny Reb,'" said the old patriarch of the library and chemical laboratory, with a smile, when the Canal Scribe found him still at the Plum street bend.

"My father came from New York to Cincinnati in the '50s by way of the Miami and Erie Canal, to survey a railroad from Covington to Louisville. We lived in Kentucky and became Confederate sympathizers. I came to Cincinnati as a boy, to work. At 15, in 1863-64, I began to fish in the canal at the Plum street bend. I worked in a drug store near there—on the site of the City Hall—and it soon was noised about that I was a 'Johnny Reb.' The Civil War was at its height and I was often pursued and whipped and driven away by the crowds of boys along the canal for being a 'Johnny Reb.'

"In those days the canal was clean and clear and I caught catfish and sunfish in it in the summer and skated upon it in the winter. The early 'packet' or passenger boats on the canal were very pretty and were nicely equipped with cabins. When my father made the trip from Toledo the canal boat stopped in a woods and the passengers landed and found a strange fruit hanging from the trees. My father had never before seen this fruit—it was the pawpaw!

"I would like to remind Cincinnatians that the man who surveyed and laid out Cincinnati was John Filson. He was murdered by Indians on one of his trips back of Cincinnati.

"Filson named the streets running east and west by number, and those running north and south after trees—as, for instance, Sycamore, Walnut, Elm. He gave the name of Filson street to what is today Plum street. That's why Plum street today ought to be called Filson street! The new boulevard could well be named in his memory.

"Years ago the politicians changed the name of the street from Filson to Plumb street—and later the 'b' was dropped. Cincinnati should revere the memory of this grand old hero of our pioneer days."

Though the canal boys whipped the diminutive and frail little John Uri Lloyd— "Johnny Reb," they called him—and often drove him from the banks of the canal sixty-five years ago, he came back and built a great pharmaceutical and chemical industry at Court and Plum streets, within a hundred feet of the fishing spot from which he had been driven by the Union boys.

There he made his many wonderful chemical inventions and discoveries, wrote the books and made researches that won him many national prizes, and there he penned "Etidorhpa," 'Stringtown on the Pike," "Red Head" and other brilliant novels. He is among our greatest canal characters. He produced wonderful works of the mind and is one of Cincinnati's brilliant ornaments.

Prof. Lloyd is a hero who ran away.

"I never fought them—I was too little—I always ran!" he exclaimed merrily, recalling those "Johnny Reb" days.

Today he still sits at the old canal site and writes and looks at seething chemicals and boiling herbs. When I called on him he was writing his autobiography and finishing a Christmas story, had a pen in one hand and a retort full of chemicals from his laboratory in the other. His assistant had just handed it to him—he was trying to find out what chemical created the strange odor of a certain compound.

Busy with his head and both hands at eighty

"Yes, they often drove me off the canal," he laughed, "and called me 'Johnny Reb.'" BUT, BOYS, HE CAME BACK!

PLUM STREET BEND WITH ITS HUGE BEER CASKS—CLUB'S ONLY "JOHNNY REB" WAS DRIVEN FROM HERE IN '63.

MOHAWK BRIDGE BALKED ON DEDICATION NIGHT

There was a lot of excitement in Mohawk nearly twenty years ago on the night that the famous old Mohawk lift bridge, shown above, was dedicated with fireworks and oratory. The bridge, with a number of passengers standing upon it, duly arose into the air, when the button was pressed—but it refused to come down. On account of some difficulty with the machinery the bridge remained suspended in the air. It had been erected at a cost of about $50,000. Major Bert L. Baldwin, consulting engineer, was called in to assist in correcting the trouble, and after certain changes were made the bridge was operated successfully for a number of years and served its purpose of reducing the steep grade of the bridge approach and offering a broader bridge roadway. It had a lift of eight feet to allow passage of the canal boats. The above picture was loaned by Harry Stangle.

Thrown Off Canal Bridge Into Icy Water on Christmas!

Aged 6 on a Christmas Day, all dolled up in my new sweater, cap and gloves Santa left the night before, I crossed Findlay street bridge on my way to show my aunt and uncle how swell I looked, when along came a smart aleck, half stewed, who thought he needed the whole bridge. He picked me up and tossed me over the bridge. Through the ice I went, sweater cap and all, but a man jumped in and saved me.—Charles Bricka, Hamilton, O.

Sausages in Boots!

I had a small raft on the canal forty-six years ago. As I was riding around with my raft an old butcher on the other side said, "Tony, bring the raft over here." I told him it would not hold him. "Bring it over," he said. As he got on my raft it sank with his weight. He waded in the water to my side of the bank and pulled off his boots to let the water out of his boots. To my surprise, water and sausages came out of those boots.—A. J. Mueller, 503 West McMicken avenue.

WALNUT ST. BRIDGE; BANNER BREWERY; CAPT. KUNTZLER'S LAST TRIP; AMERICAN BLDG. NOW TOWERS THERE.

From Age of One Capt. Kuntzler Was Reared on Canal Boat; Spent Over Forty Years on Stream

A canal boat captain himself for many years, and the son of a captain, Joseph J. Kuntzler, who loaned the two interesting pictures on adjoining pages showing canal boats in the vicinity of Walnut street, is full of the lore of the departed old stream.

Born in Cincinnati in 1871, opposite the canal bridge at Mohawk, Kuntzler was taken on board his father's boat, Oceola, when he was but a year and a half old, and, with the exception of three years at school, he was on the canal from that time until the finish of navigation on the stream. He lives at St. Bernard.

"My father had several boats, and we boated all kinds of merchandise," said Capt. Kuntzler. "We carried grain, lumber and cordwood from Toledo and Paulding County to Cincinnati. From the Wabash Canal, in upper Ohio, we brought cottonwood and delivered it to the Franklin Cotton Mills at the elbow of the canal.

"In later years I became captain and general manager of the Dayton, O., canal line, operating many boats.

"I recall when twelve to fifteen boats loaded with coal left the dock at Plum street, south of Twelfth street, for the different industries in the valley and beyond.

"Lockland, O., had three daily boat lines; Piqua had two; Minster, one; Hamilton, one daily; Middletown and Franklin one boat daily; Dayton two boats weekly. There were also many other boats, operated by the old Stone Lake Ice Company, Cincinnati Ice Company and the A. & H. Knorr Ice Company. There were also a number of independent boats hauling ice.

"Walnut and Canal street was an important canal harbor, the unloading point and office headquarters for many boat lines. There were the Middletown Canal Boat Line, owned by George B. Moore; the Lockland Line, owned by Ike Skillman; the William Dumont Line, the Buckeye, operated by the Fox Paper Company; the Hamilton Boat Line, operated by D. M. Kennedy. Farrington & Slosson operated a line from Piqua to Cincinnati, as did also others. The W. P. Orr Line carried linseed oil from the Piqua mills to Cincinnati. The boat St. Bernard ran from Minster to Cincinnati carrying pork. The boat Idaho carried grain from up-State to Cincinnati. The Cincinnati Ice Company had a score of ice boats running from their big basins 120 miles north of Cincinnati to this city. There were hundreds of canal boats carrying cord wood. Forty-five years ago I saw a string of cord wood boats reaching from Brighton to Fourteenth street.

"I operated one of the very last boats into Cincinnati in 1917, when canal business was suspended here. It was a gasoline boat—City of Dayton. I confess that tears came to my eyes as I stepped off the boat and off the dear old canal after spending more than forty happy years on its waters."

Seined With Handkerchief!

Oh, how many a good time I've had along that stretch of canal north of Liberty, just as your Times-Star article pictured it. I've seined with a handkerchief for tiny minnows along that old log bank, rode rafts and logs, rented skiffs, paddled a canoe, made bonfires, hopped on boats, including the whisky packets, stole rides on rudders and hung on to the towropes. Happy days never to be forgotten.—Charles A. Hilge, 1805 Elm.

Alonzo Kelly, an octogenarian, 1703 Baymiller street, formerly guard in Ohio State Penitentiary: I'm an old canal swimmer! Cheese it, the cop! Please enroll me.

Hello! Here's Champion Of the Mule Skinners

Mr. Charles Ludwig: The happiest days of my life were spent sitting in the saddle guiding the mules along the towpath of the Miami and Erie Canal between Cincinnati and Middletown, transporting bales of paper to the mills. I was considered the champion mule skinner of the towpath. They were driven with one line, called a "jerk line."—Monk Reichel, Princeton Hotel, city.

Joseph Sagmeister, Traction Building —No congressman ever swallowed more germs or sold more ice thrown from boats in the canal than I did.

NEAR WALNUT STREET; SKYSCRAPERS NOW GRACE SCENE; CAPT. KUNTZLER, THIRD FROM LEFT, COMMANDED FLEET.

"Out In Desert I Think of Dear Old Canal"

"Dear Mr. Ludwig: I am out here on the desert of Arizona, far from my old Cincinnati home, but my thoughts often revert back to my boyhood town and to the happy days along the dear old canal," writes Tom Woods from Tucson.

"The Canal Swimmers' Society certainly takes me back to my childhood days. We lived on Brown street, up along the canal, and it was great fun for the kids to be chased by the 'cops' along Brown street when they would catch us swimming naked, and many times I ran with my clothes in my arms and a blue coat on my trail. But I was fleet of foot and managed to get home. This was in 1870, 1871 and 1872 and until I reached the age of twelve. The old White Fence used to be my favorite swimming place. The canal was quite wide at that point. I still bear a marked finger on my right hand from getting it caught in the rudder when the man on the end was steering. That accident made me more careful."

Here we have one of the junior fishermen along the canal—it was Ray Pons, aged about 3, trying to land a whopper.

The canal swimmers will have nice weather now, for W. C. Devereaux, weather forecaster, has joined the club! "When I was a little boy I was pulled on a sled on the canal," he writes.

J. A. Elsbernd, Hyde Park—I remember the cry: "All out! Dead dog! Dead dog coming down!"

Henry Bollman, Mt. Washington—Many years ago I swam in locks between Third and Fifth streets.

Walter E. Streng, 3570 Outlook avenue: All I have to say is, "Those were the happy days."

One wintry day my brother Paul broke through the ice at Mohawk and a drunken man crawled out and saved him.—R. G. Toepfert.

Our Official Life Saver!

We propose Elmer F. Hunsicker, 3458 Vine street, as a special member of the Canal Swimmers' Society. Elmer, an expert swimmer with several rescues to his credit, is chairman of the Cincinnati Red Cross life saving unit, and is rendering a valuable service to the citizens of this community, and Elmer learned to swim in the canal. During the swimming season just closed, Elmer taught over 200 swimmers in Cincinnati how to rescue drowning persons, according to the methods of the American Red Cross.—H. S. Brutton, Cincinnati and Hamilton County Chapter, Red Cross.

Dr. Max Dreyfoos, 3325 Burnet Avenue—I skated on the canal and fell into a "suck hole."

Bill Toedt, 2941 McMicken avenue, says he fell in when a child, was taken to his grandmother's house—and "had to wear my grandmother's pajamas!"

Andy Schuman and myself were the last owners of a well-known skiff called the Sunny Side.—Leo Albert, 1573 Pullan avenue.

My grandfather, who helped build the canal, used to tell me how that old stream in the early days proved a life saver for cattle and horses during a severe drought here long ago. When the wells dried up he and others went to the canal for water for their animals.—Carl Siehl.

We used to help the men unload the sand boats and our reward was a drink of beer from the old can!—Al Bashang.

> Last Outing on Canal, Held by Freesetters
> July 27, 1917, Marked Passing of the Stream

With one brewery—Gerke's—as the point of departure, and another—Bruckmann's—as the destination, the canal boat jaunt of the Freesetters, July 27, 1917, probably the last outing ever held on the stream, was a memorable expedition to mark the passing of the canal.

"The late C. L. Doran launched the Freesetters in 1886, the name being a play on the men of that time who would sit around saloons waiting for the beer collector to make his weekly call and treat," said Edward Steinborn, city editor of the Times-Star, known as "Commonwealth" in the Freesetters—for every member has a nickname. "'Licorice' Doran was president of the society until his death. One of the first meetings of the order was held at Bruckmann's Brewery. Each member had a favorite song, and the custom was established of singing this song on the death of the member."

Thomas N. Eller, "Okay," loaned the above photograph of the farewell canal outing. The Schnapps Band provided the music, and Abe Fletcher, "Snakefeeder," famous chief chef of the Freesetters, who presided over many a function, had an ample cargo of food and refreshments on board under the awning. Mules pulled the boat out to Ludlow avenue, and the party gathered in the malt room of Bruckmann's Brewery for a happy Freesetters' function—"Snakefeeder," in his white chef's cap and coat, having prepared delicious broiled steak and pitched potatoes. A partial list of Freesetters included: August E. Rose "Mister," Charles E. Miller "Slatebreaker," William M. Bruckmann "Brewery," Supply A. Butterfield "Farmer," Moses Strauss "Mizpah," Russell Wilson "Belasco," Til Houston "Responder," C. J. Kauffman "Recklinghoosen," Bayard L. Kilgour "Hugo," John M. Klohr "Musical," Joseph Joyce "Telephone," Judge William D. Alexander "Well," Harry J. Weber "Feed," William F. Hess "Educator," Daniel Bartley "Midget," W. C. Miller "Scamp," Stanley Hart "Haynes," Robert E. Callahan "Sleuth," William A. Hopkins "Cash," Robert Kuerze "Host," E. A. Knorr "Ice," Thomas Moran "Traction," Martin O'Hara "Honest," Theo. Rosenthal "Doctor," William Reehl "Realty," Robert Saxton "Scoop," George Gutzwiler "Brockton," W. P. Rabenstein "Spotless," Dr. E. H. Thompson "Doc," Peter Lang

"Bacon," Christian Schott "Half," Joseph Sagmeister "Howdy," Joe Heintzman "Hello," Dr. A. B. Heyl "Goat," Harry Hazen "Builder," Ben A. Hulswitt "Whittaker," Dr. D. C. Handley "Bull," Louis Richter "Brass," Charles Urban "Sub," C. H. Krauss "Tulip," Charles Davis "Pop," and many others. When it was proposed to disband the Freesetters "Mister" Rose, the veteran spirit in the organization, insisted that it carry on "at least until I answer the Last Roll Call and you sing my favorite song."

Tried To Walk on Water with Air Bags Tied To His Feet and Was Nearly Drowned!

An "old timer" writes thus of a funny episode that nearly turned to tragedy: "Years ago we had an argument in a saloon in regard to Capt. Paul Boynton, who was walking on water at the time on the Ohio River. One big fellow in the crowd—he had been drinking—said, 'that was easy.' He went over to a pork house on Oliver street and got four pig bladders and tied two to each ankle. We all went to the old canal. The big boy jumped in. His head went down and his feet came up! We had a terrible time pulling him out and saving him from drowning!"

Stephen Bender, commission merchant, also tells an interesting story about how they had to save a lad who nearly drowned when he tied air-bags on his ankles:

"There was one boy in the crowd about sixteen, who could not learn to swim. He always complained he could not keep his feet up out of the water. Every boy in the neighborhood had one or two bladders from the packing houses and some would tie them under their arms, around their necks, etc., so they would learn how to swim. This particular boy brought two bladders with him and tied one around each of his ankles, and he said now he would be able to swim all right.

"He got out in the middle of the canal on a raft, started to dive into the water, and went down head first and stuck there, as the bladders kept up his feet and his head down. He wasn't able to paddle strong enough with his arms to keep his head up, and he would have been drowned if it hadn't been for a man close by who saved the boy's life by pulling him out."

Eugene A. Sigafoose comments that this suggests Shakespeare's line about "little wanton boys that swim on bladders."

Thief Threw Case of Gold Teeth Into Canal!

A thief who had stolen a case of gold-filled teeth was pursued by a policeman and at Fourteenth street the thief threw the case of teeth into the canal, so that he could run faster. We boys dove all night to recover the golden treasure, but failed to find it.—Val Cook.

"Look Out! Buffalo Bill!"

One day while playing along the canal we boys got up a spectacular engagement mimicking Indian warfare. We actually got out guns and revolvers and fired them off during this "battle." I was so scared after I fired my revolver that I threw it into the canal, and it must be there yet.—William Schaefer.

F. C. Hoffman—On a dare a friend and I went into the icy waters of the canal December 23, 1891.

"We Went Every Day If We Could Get Away!"

Oh, the fun of those happy canal days, with Phil Holzer, Charlie Schell, Victor Krauss, Otto Peuter, "Duke" Young. Our rule was: Every day—if we could get away.

And the Official Pitcher in all of our rubber baseball games was the Canal Scribe himself. Those were the happy days!—Fred Horstman, 2001 Vine street.

Ivy Lee—Grace Darling

Two famous and beautiful skiffs were the Ivy Lee, owned by John and Ed Falls, and the Grace Darling, owned by Joe and Michael Wopperer. Their boathouse, near Mohawk, later became the Clipsetta Boat Clubhouse. "My wife and I and other friends had grand times in the Ivy Lee and I taught my wife how to row!" said John Falls.

PLAYMATES OF THE TOWPATH

A FAREWELL OUTING OF 1917

The Kentucky McDowell Society, in the early summer of 1917, held an outing on the canal to help mark "Finis" on the old waterway, and Felix J. Koch, the writer, sends this photograph. This was one of the last functions on the canal, and Mr. Koch sends this description: "An old canal boat used for carrying whisky was scrubbed, draped in bunting and filled with camp stools. Light refreshments were served. There was chatting on deck, enjoying the novelty of the ride, marking the scenery, and reminiscing of canal-boat rides of long ago. Also a brief program—canal songs, by Mrs. Heflebower, Miss Weissleder and others; music of the olden time by Mrs. Blanche Greenland; poems, and a paper on old canal days by Dr. John Wilson, recollections of the canal of old by Albert Fisher, Judge Lewis Hosea and others. The mules, at the call of the muleteer, drove the laden vessel steadily upstream. Reaching a point not so far beyond Bond Hill, the passage was blocked. Crew and passengers stepped ashore and there was an old-fashioned picnic beneath the trees of a grove. By full moon the return trip to Brighton was made, and the farewell journey was done."

H. G. French's Canoe Upset!

Herbert G. French, vice president of the Procter & Gamble Company, was a canal canoeist, out in the direction of Glendale, as a boy.

"I have many happy memories of the canal," he said. "I had a canoe and paddled upon the placid canal waters—until the canoe upset, as it would do at times, and then it was a matter of making for shore and righting the craft."

Civil War Boys!

Henry Dendt, 85, Civil War veteran—I skated to Hamilton and back and played hookey from school to do it!

W. T. Baer, 83, Troy, O.—An old canal swimmer. I joined the navy at Cincinnati, sailing from there on the iron (sheet) clad Gazelle.

Robert Jones, Los Angeles, Civil War veteran—Before the Civil War I swam and skated on the canal.

C. F. Stockhoff, Gallipolis—I saw soldiers drill at Fourteenth and the canal during the Civil War.

"Oceans of Fun! Bridges Our Gymnasium! Good As Any Modern Playground!" Says Albert Kahn

"Though the canal was but a few feet wide we boys got oceans of fun out of it," commented Albert H. Kahn, treasurer of the E. Kahn's Sons Company. "That narrow strip had a heavenly length—it was more than 'miles of smiles' for us lads—miles of uproarious laughter, of unalloyed pleasure.

"We lived on Central avenue, only a block from the swimming hole, and were on the canal every day. The canal was to us boys all that the modern municipal playground, with its swimming pools, baseball diamonds and gymnastic apparatus is to the children of today. We played ball and all the other games on the towpath, had all sorts of water and ice games—and the bridges, with their iron beams and bars, were our gymnastic apparatus that you could not improve on in a playground.

"I shall never forget what a strange swimming companion I discovered next to me one day. I had gone in swimming with my brother Louis and was paddling down the middle of the stream. I noticed something swimming or floating beside me and at first thought it was another boy. But it proved to be a dead hog!

Clergyman Writes of Memories!

The pictures and stories about the old canal revive many pleasant memories of boyhood days. Swimming, boating (in a home-made flatboat), skating, and even fishing, mainly around the old haunts at St. Bernard, but often at any favorable spot between Cumminsville and Carthage—these are the boyhood pursuits which we now associate with the old stream. How fascinating it all was! We recall the old sand boats, drawn by three or four sturdy, faithful mules; then progress brought the gasoline packet boats, after that the "electric mules," and now the beautiful Central Parkway.—From the Rev. Lester E. Kemper, Lane Seminary.

Big Dog Was Swimmer, Too!

Our big black Newfoundland dog, weighing ninety pounds, was a regular canal swimmer and drove the boys out of the water. I recall that in the rag shop fire, at Findlay and Canal, several lives were lost. Recall the break in the bank of canal. The water ran down Central avenue, where we lived, and flooded the cellar. We were roused out of sleep at 2 a. m. by the police.—Bertha H. Keller and Mother.

Joseph Heuermann, 3760 Warsaw avenue: I operated last water-power mill on the canal, at Court and Broadway, and sent in a picture of the old mill.

Henry Delfendahl, 523 Slack street: Eighty years ago I swam across the canal under the Sycamore bridge.

Seein' Things at Night!

We "stood on the bridge at midnight,"
  Me and my old pal,
"And the moon rose over the city,"
  And shone in the old canal.

My pal insisted strenuously,
  He saw TWO moons quite clear,
But at Kissel's and at Schuman's
  He had had a lot of beer.
    —E. M. Nixon, Westfield, Ind.

First Boat—Black Diamond

My grandfather, William H. Woodruff, owned the grocery at Canal and Race, southeast corner, for forty-five years. Grandfather was a business associate of the Hon. Benjamin Eggleston, and he also owned the first canal boat that floated in the Miami canal. It was named the Black Diamond. My dog used to retrieve sticks thrown into the canal. I fell off a canal boat one day and my uncle rescued me. Crossing the canal on an errand, I picked up a stone to throw in, but by mistake held on to the stone and, instead, threw the silver coins, wrapped in paper, into the canal!—Mrs. Lida W. Bart.

My father was one of the pioneer packers of Camp Washington and I lived at the canal shore fifty years—1867 to 1917. Lived twenty-eight years at the Brighton House. The rear of that building faced the canal.—Mrs. Alma Alexander Abacherli.

THE CANAL AT ST. BERNARD—PHOTO BY ELMER L. FOOTE.

Ouch!

I lived near the old canal at Carthage. We boys owned a motor boat with which we could be found anywhere between Lockland and Cincinnati. Our favorite sport was hanging onto the rudders of the old boats. On one occasion a mule driver lashed us with his blacksnake whip for hanging on. The next time he came down the boys stoned him. We never saw him after that.—"Bill" Huber.

Aha! A Rock Thrower!

If you have such a subdivision I am eligible for the rock throwers.—Wm. H. Emerson.

While operating my drug store here in Long Beach, Cal., my thoughts go back to the old canal, where I played tin-can shinney, swam, skated and fell in, all so happily.—Lawrence E. Creeden, Long Beach.

Fleet of Canal Boats To Civil War Meeting

Our crowd swam above Lockland, where the banks were lined with beautiful trees. Here we would plunge into the sparkling water, from the stern of the boat, and mingle with the geese and ducks that spent their time along the grassy banks. We selected this locality because the water was fresh and clear, while south of Lockland the water was tainted from the waste from mills.

We loved to swim along—

Those sunny slopes and beechen swell,
Where the shadowed light of evening fell.

It was about the time of the last year of the Civil War that the majority of the people of Lockland engaged a fleet of canal boats and journeyed to Carthage Fair Grounds to attend a great political meeting. — Anson McKinney, former school principal.

Armleder Built "Greatest Bonfire" In 1876!

"By a strange fate every decade of my life drew me back to the canal," said Otto Armleder, retired manufacturer. "We lived at Court and Elm and had a huge Newfoundland dog that would bring back sticks we threw in the canal. One day father threw in a stick as a wooden door happened to be floating by—and the big dog swam back with the door! At ten I bought an old skiff, calked it up and made money renting it out at 25 cents an hour. Also owned the only racing shell-boat, with outrigger oars, that I ever saw on the canal.

"My mother, an ardent Democrat, wanted me to build a big bonfire for the Tilden parade during the memorable Tilden-Hayes Presidential campaign in 1876. I got three great casks from in front of Lamping's soap factory on the canal, and many salt barrels from the canal porkhouses. We piled the three greasy casks on each other—fifteen feet high—and it made the 'greatest bonfire ever seen in Cincinnati,' so the newspapers said the next day. But the fire broke all the windows and burned all the paint off our house! And besides, mother paid Lamping $6 for the casks! But she was so pleased with the 'greatest bonfire' for her candidate, that she was satisfied to pay the bills! I boxed Peter Nolan, local heavyweight champion, on the banks of the canal, where we often had amateur matches.

"In 1880 I came back to the canal—operating a beer bottling plant where the Y. M. C. A. is now located. In 1904 I again came back to the canal, starting my carriage and later truck factory in the old Haydock carriage works, Canal and Twelfth streets." The building is seen on the next page.

Mr. Armleder was there for twenty-five years, having just retired. One day a boy fell off the Twelfth street bridge. Mr. Armleder, seeing a crowd, rushed from his office, leaped into the water and pulled out the lad—but it was too late. Mr. Armleder was a leader in the Fall Festivals held along the canal. In 1906 he launched the canal subway movement before a meeting of the Central City Association.

The picture on the opposite page, loaned by the H. Nieman Company, 1031 John street, tells of the last days on the canal. It shows the last canal boat being removed by the Cincinnati Transfer Company to the Ohio River, where it was sold to a firm in upper Illinois. Herbert Nieman, president of the H. Nieman Company, and Louis Hock, president of the Cincinnati Transfer Company, the latter shown in the foreground of the picture, used to swim in this same spot. "Herb" Nieman, who later became an amateur champion swimmer of Ohio, says that this is where he got his start.

He Saw Angels!

We had a diving board stuck under the electric mule tracks. A fellow ran after me to tag me, and just as I dove off the board it broke and I went down and hit bottom head first in the mud, and there I stayed until they pulled me out! I never saw so many pretty angels in my life.—Charles F. Danker.

I have picked wild flowers and gathered pussy willows on the banks of the canal above Lockland. I have admired the beauty of the quiet stream through the fields and along the roadways.—Stella Johnson Johnston (teacher).

Aaron Block—I was born in 1862 at Eighth and Broadway in a house built over the canal, the water running underground and beneath the home.

Saved by Belle of Nelson!

"I fell through the ice while skating in bitter cold weather in 1886, and a bottle of Belle of Nelson whisky saved my life," said A. E. Burkhardt. "Nearly frozen, I was taken to uncle Erkenbrecher's starch factory and my clothing was taken off and dried in the furnace room. I was put to bed at home and the doctor said that bottle, brought by men at the factory, saved my life."

William Kuhr—As a child I often saw the fire department called out to rescue a hog or cow, from a drove, that fell into the canal. And once I fell in, too, was submerged and nearly drowned. But boatmen saw my uplifted hand and rescued me.

LAST CANAL BOAT BEING LIFTED OUT OF CANAL—PHOTO FROM THE H. NIEMAN COMPANY.

E. P. Bradstreet, 99, Oldest Member, Reminisces

E. P. Bradstreet, 99, retired attorney of Hartwell, a founder of the Cincinnati Gym and Associated Charities and oldest living Yale graduate, is the oldest member of our society. He defeated Lincoln in a game of chess before the Civil War.

"Canals were a vital business factor when I came here in 1854," he writer. "I recall the canal boats passing to and from the river. Canal street was lined with commission houses. We were ahead of Chicago then. The canal water was clear and made beautiful waterfalls at the locks. In 1854 I saw a fire in a warehouse on the canal.

"There was confusion and delay because of trouble between the volunteer and paid fire departments. But suddenly a tall, fine-looking man—a leader—appeared with an ax. The crowd cheered him. Mounting to the roof, he cut a hole in it and applied a stream of water. The fire at once began to die out. That man was Miles Greenwood—a name Cincinnati should revere forever."

Canal Boat Campaigners Greeted With Brickbats

During the Garfield Presidential campaign our Republican Club, with torchlights and red shirts and Glee Club, marched over to the Dodsworth Distillery. We all got on the old whisky boat Rialto and went to town to hear, I think, President Garfield speak at the old Galt House. As we were passing under the Mohawk bridge someone who had placed a row of bricks on the railing pushed them over on us. We were packed on tight, standing up on the boat, and when one of the bricks hit you you just had to sink down. I remember Jim Cable was standing alongside of me and went down. But that did not prevent us from going on to our political meeting.

When swimming in the canal we used to jump on the canal boat rudders—until one day I did that and found the rudder full of pointed tacks! That kept us off!—Armand W. de Serisy, Cumminsville.

College President Pinched!

John M. Steinfeldt, founder and president of the San Antonio, Tex., College of Music, writes:

"I still have a canal mark on my pianistic fingers. When on my way to school I stopped with other lovers of wonderful old Fourteenth street bridge to lave in sluggish waters, feeling in the sides for crawfish and pulling out of the hole a big one which had attached itself on the tip of my middle finger."

I swam in the canal, but sometimes there was not enough dirt in it to hold me up, so father took me to Robert Schmidt's Floating Bath Emporium in the Ohio River. The most exciting events were the annual canal boat picnics of our church. On one of these trips a woman became hysterical and had to be restrained from jumping into the water.—F. W. Strubbe.

A bulldog pulled me into the canal one day, clothes and all.—Samuel Doersam.

From Central America

From distant Cape Haitien, Haiti, Mrs. B. F. Scherffius writes: "Cincinnati was the city of my birth, and often, as a child, I would sit on the canal bank and be thrilled to watch the boats go by. Next summer, on my vacation home, I will follow the whole canal route!" Louis C. Warner, Canal Zone, Panama: "I had many happy experiences on the canal." Bill Berwanger writes from Havana, Cuba: "Just met T. G. Lunken of Birmingham here and he is an old Cincinnati canal swimmer."

Beginning in 1860, my father boated on the canal thirty-eight years. He was lock tender at Lockland in 1913. Albert Lindsay and Harve Pauley of Lockland are among the oldest veteran canal boatmen.—Anna Aylward King, Milwaukee.

None of the swimmers have yet reported anything about the leeches that would get on us in the canal and that we would pick off our bodies.—Dr. C. Friedrich.

ARTIST'S DREAM OF 1884 THAT HAS COME TRUE!

This picture was copied from a Cincinnati weekly, the Graphic, of September 27, 1884, and shows the early hopes for transforming the canal into a subway and boulevard. The artist did not foresee the automobile—but he did not miss his guess much. The reality of today looks much like the dream of forty-five years ago. The picture was loaned by Robert H. Doepke, vice president of the Alms & Doepke Company.

"One day, when I was a boy, one of our wagons, laden with Easter bonnets for the ladies of Mt. Auburn and the hilltops, was accidentally backed into the canal and upset," said Mr. Doepke. "I will never forget the sad spectacle of those Easter hats floating down the canal. They were all lost—and the good ladies had to go without their new Easter hats next day."

I recall how the Laurel street crowd would take their exercise by throwing Issy and Dave Sternberg into the canal.—Benjamin Hirsch.

Seventy-five years ago—in 1854, as a little girl—I rode on the canal in my skiff, and how I loved the old stream.—Mrs. Wellington Arnold.

Has any canal swimmer related how we hated to have anybody crack rocks together under water when we swam?—C. J. John.

G. W. Yates, Loth street, saved a lad of six from drowning in 1919, just before the canal "went dry"—probably the last canal rescue.

"I Wouldn't Exchange Canal Pleasures for Any Of Today! World of Innocent Fun, Morn to Night!"

"Dear Friend and Classmate—I am happy to learn that so many other children, outside of those of my own crowd around Music Hall, enjoyed the pleasures offered by the dear old canal," writes Mrs. Louisa Munz Philipps, proprietor of the Philipps' Swimming Pools, whose son and daughter have both distinguished themselves as champion swimmers and have each won scores of swimming medals.

"The towpath playmates were one great family, sharing each other's joys and sorrows. Jealousy and hatred were unknown. My only regret was that I wasn't born a boy and join in plunging into the cool waters. We had to be satisfied loaning handkerchiefs to the boys to dry their hair for fear of being invited to the 'woodshed' upon arriving home with wet heads.

"The Peerless Athletic Club, 1528 Plum street, practically lived 'on the sea shore!' What thrills we experienced by being invited by George Schneider, now captain of the Bond Hill fire department, to take a row up to Brighton. He would pack twelve children or more in a row boat and row up and down the canal until dark.

"I wouldn't exchange the joyous experiences of my childhood along the canal for any of the pleasures of today, as we lived in a world of innocent recreation and fun from morn until night—thanks to the dear old canal."

A Few More Heroes!

"I saved the life of a boy," writes Henry Wellman. Mrs. William Rosenzweig lost her hat but saved her baby sister from drowning. John W. Knosp saved the lives of two boys at Liberty street. George Lichtenfels saved a boy from drowning in front of the old sand house. Elsa Hardung Everly pulled her girl friend out when she fell through the ice. And there were hundreds of other rescues.

Earl Gerhart and Catherine and Henry Strobel skating at First Basin. Bates's Woods in background. Photo from Mrs. Margaret Bohnenkamp.

Steered Pocahontas at 8

Neil C. Sullivan, 80, writes from Longmont, Col.: "At the age of 12 I steered the canal boat Pocahontas—saw as many as 200 boats plying the canal. St. Mary's Reservoir, that fed the canal, was the largest artificial body of water in the world. At every lock the power was used to drive mills. Coal from river barges was shoveled into canal boats when the canal flowed into the river years ago. I can swim and dive good as ever!"

Judge Darby Was Rescued!

"I, too, am a canal boy," said Judge Thomas Darby, "was rescued from drowning, like most others, and took part in juvenile battles as a member of the Brightons."

In 1847, when I was 6 years old, a local swimming champion named Walsh picked me up and threw me into the canal. That was eighty-two years ago.— John Rogers, 88, theatrical manager, formerly of Woods Theater, Cincinnati.

From Howard Thurston, the magician: "Over forty-five years ago, when I ran away from home at Columbus as a boy of ten and came to Cincinnati, I used to swim in the old canal and have many pleasant recollections of that stream."

SWIMMING HOLE CONCRETE NOW! SUBWAY AT WADE STREET.

This Boy Got a Kiss!

Our crowd, pursued by another, fled over the Vine street bridge. I was left alone and had to jump in the canal and swim across with my clothes on. My crowd was waiting at my home to see me get a spanking, but when I told my mother how my gang ran away from me she went outside with me and kissed me right in front of all the boys!—Albert B. Sherer, past president Central Vine Street Business Association.

Ah! They Owned Canal!

Jack Dwyer—I belonged to the old Eighth street gang. We owned the canal from Court street to the river! At least we thought we did—till driven out by some other crowd!

A woman writes: "While boating with my sweetheart in Cumminsville, his oar struck an obstruction and we found it to be the body of a woman who had ended her life."

Prohibition Leader in, Too!

Madison F. Larkin, Scranton, Pa., former Prohibition candidate for United States senator from Pennsylvania, is an old canal swimmer. He writes that he was pushed into the canal at Cincinnati when he was a small boy in 1861, and managed to paddle and keep up until rescued. He adds:

"This all took place back of the old Nathaniel Ropes & Co. candle factory on Lock street, between little Fourth and Fifth streets. After the occurrence I was a regular swimmer in the canal."

Albrecht F. Leue, superintendent Loveland, O., Schools—The canal days were wonderful. But we also used to swim in Millcreek, in the "bottomless" hole at Arlington street. When the trunk sewer cleans up Millcreek let's have another celebration.

John Wartmann—I recall the drowning of a boy at the old P. & G. plant fifty years ago.

Girl's Odd Fish Story! Catfish She Caught in Family Coffee Pot Were Cooked with the Coffee!

Mrs. Ella Cochran of Newport tells this unusual fish yarn:

"My godmother had a store on Main street, near the canal, and I remember how her daughter and I would take the nice clean coffee and tea strainer and one of her mother's biggest glass bowls and slip away to the canal and catch little fish with the strainer and sell them to other children for pretty buttons. One day we took the coffee pot and put our fish in it, but in our hurry to get it back before someone caught us we left a catfish, and in came godmother, put the water in to boil and soon the coffee. Neither of us had the nerve to tell her or had a chance to pour the coffee out. But at the table first the "Mr." and then the "Mrs." sniffed the coffee—again and again. Catching the two of us winking, we were taken to task and 'owned up'."

Alluring Canal Boats!

In my early youth, about 1870-1873, my daily road to and from the old Tenth District School on Vine street led me over the Twelfth street canal bridge. We would look down on the boats as they passed underneath, and how alluring they looked! The little end cabin, with its cute windows and white curtains, and its little pet dog either barking or lying soundly asleep in the sun on the deck!—Mrs. Joana Eppens Smith, teacher, Hillcrest School.

And who can recall Wienerwurst Mike of blessed memory and our old friend the cop—red-headed Barney Rakel?—L. E. Peterson.

In front of the Edison plant, in 1902, I went diving for the body of Howard Payne. After taking him from his watery grave, the crowd that lined both banks went wild with cheers.—Thomas Winter.

She Hunted Crawdads!

Even if my mother wouldn't let me go in the water (which I did) I couldn't do such a mild thing as throwing sticks or stones in the water like other girls, because it was much more thrilling hunting for crawdads!—Opal Mason.

The cops found me on the canal when I was lost at the age of three. That was my first experience with the "watch on the Rhine"—the cops on the canal.—William Boehle.

After all kinds of happy experiences on the canal, I wish to nominate my brother, Capt. W. B. Havlin, for the position of Grand Canal Boat Jumper!—J. L. Havlin, Nelsonville, O.

A friend writes: "The late Commodore H. Lee Brooks, who was head of the Coney Island Company and president of the Chamber of Commerce, was a canal swimmer and came from Vermont to Cincinnati with his mother and brothers in 1848 on a canal boat."

WINTER SCENE IN CUMMINSVILLE—PHOTO LOANED BY MRS. CATHERINE HEYN.

THE LAST TRICKLE UNDER THE VINE STREET BRIDGE THAT LED INTO THE "OVER-THE-RHINE" REGION.

Nearly Every Business Man Has Canal Yarn!

Nearly every business man in Cincinnati swam or skated on the canal or has some sort of canal yarn to tell.

"As boys, did any of you play along the canal?" I asked some well-known business men at the Cincinnati Club and Chamber of Commerce, and in a moment there gathered friendly and enthusiastic groups exchanging thrilling canal reminiscences.

"My heart goes pitapat every time I motor by my old swimming hole," one exclaimed. Morris Wickersham told of happy skating parties; F. L. Garrison of how he swam on a plank at ten; Frederick Hertenstein of a skiff ride and rescue; Percy Hooe of entertaining the visiting merchants "Over-the-Rhine;" F. W. Garber of jolly and thrilling canal episodes; Charles Urban of swimming and boating; Eugene Buss of aiding the playmate who "flowed" over the overflow at the aqueduct; Leo J. Van Lahr of skating till exhausted; Paul Verkamp of canal boat riding; J. E. Fitzpatrick of swimming at the old hospital; Charles L. Shannon, Jr., of paying 15 cents to fish all day in a canal basin; Bert Baldwin of the German Village on the canal at the Fall Festival. A. G. Muhlhauser swam at Rialto, Ed Voss was paddled for "going in" and Julian Pollak broke through the ice and had a long walk home. Oscar Gassman "swam every night." Frank Santry was a skater and Harry Phillips played on canal boats. A. P. Strietmann learned to swim near the aqueduct and Dr. Moses Salzer skated and helped his brother who fell in. Phil Geier broke through the ice at Second Basin. A. G. Schwartz killed a water snake that was swallowing a catfish out on the canal bank—and the fish was saved and swam away! Vincent Beckman, John Brewster, August Wisser, Joe Oberly, Arthur O. Evans and Ed F. Romer qualified as skaters of speed and skill. Louis G. Pochat swam back of the Music Hall. William Licht had worlds of fun on the stream. Edward Herschede and Charles Murray played and swam in it as lads. J. J. Castellini fell in at Vine street. Thomas W. Burke liked to drop from the bridges. Ed A. Muller fell in near Wade street—and his crowd of canal singers sang like Italian gondoliers. David G. Devore, president of the Rotary Club, liked the skating parties that included charming girls. Harry Price and Charles Wachtel told of picnics beyond the Clifton woods. J. J. Schmidt fell through while skating. Monroe Izor, 82, had many happy canal stories, and so the pleasant reminiscences went on and on, everyone having a story to tell.

Canal Boat Sank in Seventy Feet of Water!

"About fifty years ago the canal boat North America sank in seventy feet of water in a former gravel pit near the aqueduct over Millcreek," said W. A. Gregg, 76, Cincinnati collector of canal tolls, rents and fines from 1894 to 1908. "I recall the steam canal boat that plied up the canal from the Ohio River to Canal street seventy years ago to transfer freight from canal to river. We had a gauge in the canal at our State office, near Main street, and the water varied in depth only three or four inches. The drop in the 'twelve-mile level'—Lockland to Cincinnati—was only an inch to the mile! Canal boats registered fifty to seventy tons. A few side-wheel canal steamers were built at Lockland. Has anybody mentioned the terrible boiler explosion in a factory on the canal above Findlay street fifty years ago? I saw the piece of boiler that was hurled four blocks and killed two children. Years ago, when there was keen rivalry between the various passenger boats to Toledo, each boat had a 'horn blower.' For an hour before the boats left from Main street these 'horn blowers' blew and concertised, each trying to outdo the others in volume of sound and melody to attract passengers. Near by were a number of hotels that prospered in the old days on the canal trade."

I received one cent, when a little boy, for drowning a sack full of cats in the canal.—Charles G. Scherer.

My first invitation from a young man was to go ice-skating on the canal at Second Basin.—Mrs. Martha Vogel.

BOYS PLAYING IN LAST POOL, AT ELM STREET, TEN YEARS AGO WHEN CANAL WAS EMPTIED—BOONE PHOTO.

Three Great Parades Marked Parkway Dedication

Tens of thousands of canal swimmers and others took part in the great three-day celebration, October 1, 2 and 3, 1928, marking the dedication of the new Central Parkway, along the route of the old towpath.

Attorney Frank H. Freericks, who played on the canal banks as a child, and was a pioneer in the movement for the boulevard, was president of the Central Parkway Dedication Citizens' Committee, composed of representatives of approximately 150 civic, business and fraternal organizations. Robert H. Doepke was vice president; Frank J. Weller, secretary, and D. C. Keller, treasurer. The Executive Board included these, with Frank L. Raschig, C. E. Richter, Charles Theodore Greve, Charles S. Cowie, Judge William H. Lueders, former Judge Coleman Avery, Col. William C. Meyer, James G. Strobridge, Judge Frederick L. Hoffman, William H. Miller and Charles Eisen. Ned S. Hastings was managing director, and Rudolph Benson director of publicity. The first day was Civic and Governmental Day, with Judge Avery chairman. Young Cincinnati Day was observed the second day, with Judge Hoffman chairman. The third day was Fraternal Day, and Judge Lueders was chairman. Col. Meyers was chairman of the General Parade Committee. Inspiring was the Parade of Youth on the second day. With a historical pageant, Mr. Greve acting as chairman, John C. Weber, veteran canal swimmer, once more led his famous military band. The formal dedicatory exercises on Monday, October 1, were preceded by a luncheon at the Chamber of Commerce, at which H. C. Blackwell, president of the chamber, was host. The dedication was held at the Courthouse, Mr. Freericks presiding. Addresses were made by George Puchta, former mayor of Cincinnati; Mayor Murray Seasongood, Lieut. Gov. William G. Pickrell, E. W. Edwards, president of the Board of Rapid Transit Commissioners, and Frederick W. Chatfield, acting president of the Board of Park Commissioners. Mr. Edwards formally transferred the Parkway to the Park Commission. Tributes were paid to Irwin M. Krohn, president of the Park Commission, and L. A. Ault, former president, who were ill and unable to attend. The Civic and Governmental Day parade followed, and soldiers, police and fire departments, post-office employes and county employes participated. A feature of this magnificent procession was the transportation pageant. More than 50,000 people saw the Civic and Governmental Day parade, and even larger crowds viewed the Parade of Youth and Fraternal Parades on the two days following. At the beginning of the first day's parade, a bomb, lighted to signal the parade to start, exploded in the crowd, causing slight injuries to five persons and giving Joseph Sagmaster of the Times-Star a busy hour. Twenty thousand children, from public and parochial schools, Boy Scouts and Camp Fire Girls, took part in the Parade of Youth the second day. The Historical Pageant featured fifty ornate floats, and was the most pretentious thing of the kind attempted in recent years. The Fraternal Parade, on the evening of October 3, was the concluding feature. In the line-up were various organizations, among them the United Spanish War Veterans and their women's auxiliaries, the Army and Navy Union, Veterans of Foreign Wars, Disabled American War Veterans, American Legion, the "Forty and Eight," Syrian Temple, Nobles of the Mystic Shrine; Oola Khan Grotto, Knights of Pythias, Pythian Sisters, Loyal Order of Moose, Modern Woodmen of America, Independent Order of Odd Fellows, Foresters of America, Improved Order of Red Men, Knights of St. John, the Catholic Order of Foresters, the Knights of Columbus, Patriarchs Militant, Rebekahs, Calvary Clifton Lodge, F. and A. M., the German Beneficial Union, the American Hellenic Educational Progressive Association, the North Cincinnati Gymnasium, and Cincinnati Aerie No. 142, Fraternal Order of Eagles.

"The old Cincinnati Ice Company, of which my father was president, harvested ice from Second Basin, Mummert's, Dietz's Basin, Ross and Chester Lakes, and lakes at Port Union, Fairfield, Hamilton and all the way up to Troy," said James Cullen, president of the City Ice and Fuel Company. "The company had twenty to thirty ice houses, with a capacity of 200,000 tons. The ice was marked in twenty-two-inch squares and 'plowed,' or cut by horses. A fleet of about ten boats hauled the ice to Cincinnati, and one of the happiest moments of my life was when my father told me, as a boy, that a boat, the James Cullen, had been named after me! Sam Blair was a pioneer ice man, and his grandson, Lester Blair, is still in the business with us. The Knorr and the Stone Lake were other early ice companies on the canal. Knorr cut ice at Lesourdsville Lake, now a pleasure resort."

CENTRAL PARKWAY DEDICATION OCT. 1, 1928; CROWD AT COURTHOUSE—PHOTO BY JOSEPH BANFORD.

Additional Members of Canal Swimmers' Society

Here are additional names of members of Cincinnati's famous Canal Swimmers' Society—the only organization of its kind in the world, whose membership includes men and women of all ranks, workmen and employers, the mayor of Cincinnati, governor of Ohio, members of Congress, the speaker of the House of Representatives, and a former President of the United States and the present Chief Justice of the United States. It was impossible to print all of the vast number of letters received. All in the list below sent interesting letters, loaned pictures, or otherwise contributed to the success of the society, and the Canal Scribe here expresses his gratitude to all.

FROM CINCINNATI AND VICINITY

Daniel Angert
Anne L. Anderson
J. H. Androit
Alma Abaecherli
William Adams
James Agnew
George P. Albert
Leo Albert
Harry E. Alberts
Henrietta Amon
Frank Aneshansel
James A. Anderson
T. H. Anderson
Cecil Appelblatt
Wm. Appelmann
Carl Albertz
Henry Alexander
E. H. Albertz
E. E. Armbrust
Mrs. W. Arnold
Frank R. Arnold
Butz Arnold
Mrs. Fannie Ash
Clara M. Aspenleiter
John C. Aspenleiter
Herman Bumiller
Adolph "Bube" Kistler
Earl Burwell
A. J. Braunwart
Mrs. Elizabeth Braegger
Carl Berling
Louis E. Ballus
John H. Bittner
M. J. Braegger
The Rev. Emil E. Baum
John H. Bittner
Sam Bayer
Henry D. Bollman
Louis E. Boluss
Henry Behrle, Jr.
Stephen Bender
Thomas W. Burke
C. J. Boos
Homer and Helen Biedenbach
Henry Birkemeyer
M. J. Bramble, Jr.
Dr. A. J. Bauman
William Bailer
John P. Baumann
Herman Bamberger
Al Bashang
Mrs. Lida Bart
Mrs. W. L. Bart
Thomas E. Bart
D. M. Bartlett
George G. Baetz
J. F. Behringer
Martin Behrle
Douglas Beckham
Walter W. Becky
Charles H. Behrle
Henry Behrle, Sr.
Wilford Beringer
Fred Bernhardt
E. J. Berry
Louis Berger
Charles Bertram
Marie Bender
Fred Bentel

FROM OUT OF TOWN

Ph. C. Abbihl, Arlington, N. J.
Mrs. Anna Aylward King, Milwaukee.
George T. Alter, Chicago.
Henry D. Barth, Springfield, O.
W. A. Behrle, Hamilton, Canada.
William H. Berning, Chattanooga.
W. T. Baer, Troy, O.
August Bode Luckey, Seattle.
Lawrence Creeden, Long Beach, Cal.
Jake Levy, California.
Mr. and Mrs. W. L. Curnayn, Haines City, Fla.
George Carlson, Cedar Rapids, Ia.
Mrs. J. A. Cunningham, Lafayette, Ala.
C. A. Daniel, Chicago.
James A. Doherty, Toledo, O.
Anthony Faderle, Chicago, Ill.
James G. Falls, Fayetteville, O.
Alex Frankel, Lima, O.
Emil Goldschmidt, Sunman, Ind.
Charles Stockhoff, Gallipolis, O.
J. C. Georgi, Ashland, Ky.
L. E. Gebhart, Dayton, O.
V. E. Grotlisch, Washington, D. C.
A. W. Grotlisch, Des Moines, Ia.
Herman Haerlin, Dayton, O.
Bertha S. Hyman, New York.
Fred J. Heintz, Lexington, Ky.
John J. Hauss, St. Marys, O.
Herbert R. Hopkins, St. Louis.
George W. Johanning, Batesville, Ind.
John Kramer, Los Angeles.
Dr. Elmer E. Kimmel, Miamisburg, O.
Matt F. Larken, Scranton, Pa.
Mrs. Alfred Madonna, Philadelphia.
Dr. William H. Mueller, Orlando, Fla.
Charles Nieman, Hollywood, Cal.
Ed M. Nixon, Westfield, Ind.
Alban J. Norris, Detroit.
Walter H. Reynolds, Liberty, Ind.
Mrs. Maud Rolph, Hamersville, O.
Aug. Scheiffele, Lakeland, Fla.
Mrs. Minnie Doppler Sheppard, Yorba Linda, Cal.
Agugust Scheiffele, Lakeland, Fla.
Mrs. Edna Schmid, Philadelphia.
Peter B. Steil, Sunman, Ind.
Frank E. Stevenson, Los Angeles.
Mrs. B. F. Scherffius, Cape Haitien, Haiti.
Charles T. Schneider, Marietta, O.
Dr. J. M. Steinfeldt, San Antonio, Tex.
Theodore Schaum, Washington, D. C.
Leroy J. Schwenkmeyer, San Diego, Cal.
W. T. Selzer, Pittsburgh.
F. W. Tech, Bedford, Ind.
A. C. Sinks, Tippecanoe City, O.
T. Albood, Tucson, Ariz.
Will and Ed Tech, North Vernon, Ind.
Gus Truman, Lafayette, Ind.
Dr. E. B. Vincent, Sunman, Ind.
William Volkert, Cleveland, O.
Ed Volkert, New York.
George W. Wurster, Lakeland, Fla.
Harry Warnock, Ft. Recovery, O.
Louis C. Warner, Canal Zone, Panama.
C. L. Weber, North Vernon, Ind.
J. O. Wright, Green Cove Springs, Fla.
Harry B. Weir, Milwaukee.
Clifford F. Weber, Detroit.

FROM CINCINNATI AND VICINITY

Carl W. Beckwith
C. A. Benninger
E. B. Beresford
Mrs. Marg't Beresford
William Boehle
Ben Binkert
Frank Biedenbach
Francis M. Biddle
Aaron Block
Earl Blersch
Alma Blattner
W. C. Bold
Louis Botzing
Albert Boland
Edwin Boeschlin
M'garet Bohnenkamp
Edward Bohnenkamp
A. P. Boeckley
Rudolph Boeschlin
Wm. Bossemeyer
Cornelius Bos
Mrs. Marg't Bockway
John Boswell
William Boehle
J. C. Brech
Dr. C. J. Broeman
William Bruckmann
John R. Bryan
Joseph Breining
Harry S. Brutton
Elizabeth Braunecker
Mrs. Lena Brestel
William Brodhagen
Charles Bricka
Mrs. Mathilda Brandt
Harry Bradbury
Harry M. Bridwell
G. F. Brossart
Andreas E. Burkhardt
Charles Buehler
William Butz
Mrs. William Butz
A. Bywaters
John Cantzler
Dr. L. S. Colter
Frank Crippner
Emil Calme
Joseph J. Castellini
Jimmy Cantzler
L. Christoffel
Samuel Chalfie
Gray Coleman
John R. Cooling
Mrs. Ella Cochran
Carl Conradi
J. F. Cullman
C. J. Currus
Judge Thos. H. Darby
J. Henry Doppes
Bill and Ray DeWitt
Dr. Max Dreyfoos
Arthur W. Davis
Henry Delfendahl
M. A. Daly
Charles F. Danker
M. W. Davis
D. J. Davis
E. A. Dartnall
David Davis
J. L. Davis
Carl Delin
W. C. Devereaux
Mrs. Mary Desch

PLAYMATES OF THE TOWPATH

20,000 CHILDREN IN DEDICATION PARADE.

A. W. DeSerisy
Jacob Dewald
W. J. Devine
C. H. Dillman
John Dinkelaker
Herbert Dinkelaker
Edward Dickmeier
Walter S. Dixon
Raymond J. Dierker
Joseph T. Dilhoff
Fred W. Donner
Mrs. Sarah Downey
Mrs. Lizzie Dorsch
Samuel Doersam
Emma Dollman
Mrs. E. L. Donnelly
Fred Doiling, Jr.
Joe Dressman
William H. Drach
Dr. W. F. Dupper
George Dubach
William F. Dunkman
J. R. Duncan
Arthur Etter
J. A. Elsbernd
William Eisenecher
Mrs. Eisenecher
William H. Emerson
Morton O. Ewing
Frank K. Eastman
Mark Eastman
John M. Eisman
Albert Eilers
Harry J. Ell
Mrs. Gertie Enth
Mary Engeln
Joseph D. Engelbert
Frank Ernst
William Ernst
George Ernst
Charles O. Espich
Elsa H. Everly
Louis Ezekiel
Mrs. George Preson
Joe Franken
Chas. Franken
Sam Franken
Edw. Franken
Robert Franken
Milton Franken
John Fasold

G. A. Fleischmann
R. M. Fleming
George R. Falls
Ernst Henry Faey
Joseph Farrell
J. Harry Fathauer
Bert Fagin
A. L. Fancher
Mrs. Frank Faller
Frank Faller
Miss Emma Farber
John Fath
Albert Fath
George Fasold
Charles Fehrman
Charles W. Fehrmann
A. H. Finke
George Fitzpatrick
Norma J. Fischer
Chas. Finkelstein
A. L. Fillmore
Mrs. A. L. Fillmore
Charles Fisher
F. P. Fish, Sr.
Harry E. Fisk
Marion Floyd
Conrad J. Fleig, Sr.
Robert Flick
C. H. Flohr
Mrs. L. Flaig
R. M. Fleming
L. A. Fortwangler
Samuel Fopman
Clifford R. Fox
William Frank
Edward Frank
Carl Prietsch
Edward Frohliger
Dr. O. Friedrich
Harry Franke
George H. Froelich
L. W. Fritsche
Pat Furey
Charles M. Funk
J. E. Fulweiler
A. V. Fuhrman
George Geist
W. F. Gross
Stephen Gerrard
Gustave E. Gebhart
G. H. Grothus

Geo. A. J. Gampfer
William H. Greer
Ed Gelke
Walter G. Garber
D. S. Gaddis
Henry J. Gade
Louis Gassner
M. D. Gall
C. J. Garttmann
E. W. Geiss
Frank Gerding
Arthur L. Gerhold
Charles Gick
Mrs. E. Gloystein
Harry Gordon
Levi C. Goodale
F. M. Goble
M. D. Goetz
Fred Grimmer
Martha E. Greenfield
Mrs. N. Grueninger
O. M. Gray
Katherine Grotlisch
W. A. Gregg
John C. Groene
W. L. Gross
Frank Grey
Alfred T. Gray
Mrs. Elizabeth Hartman
John Hillen
Victor Henke
Carrie Hugo
Mike Hockstuck
Congressman William E. Hess
Mr. and Mrs. Ed Hempelman
Dr. H. H. Hines
W. E. Haller
Fred Wm. Husman
George Hildeman
Albert D. Hildwein
C. H. Hill
Jack Hagedorn
Geo. H. Hindersman
Phil F. Harten
Sarah Hirst
William J. Hart
Harry A. Happe
E. S. Howard

Jack Huber
F. C. Hoffman
George F. Hilgeman
George H. Haller
Charles Hardig
John Hardig
George C. Hammann
Arthur G. Hall
W. B. Harrison
Ditty Hayes
Edward Hauschildt
C. H. Harris
Reinhardt Hascher
J. L. Havlin
Mrs. Lena Habbel
W. H. H. Harrison
Ruth Hageman
William Hageman
Louis C. Hahn, Sr.
Mrs. Addie B. Hauer
W. A. Hastie
William A. Haug
R. P. Hargitt
Thekla Hablitzel
Dr. W. D. Haines
Oscar Hausser
W. E. Haller
Olga Hablitzel
S. J. Hauser
H. A. Haller
Clifford Harris
W. A. Hastie
Mrs. Addie B. Hauer
Richard Hartfield
Frank R. Harding
R. F. Hagaman
Harry Hagaman
Joseph Heuermann
John Heisler
Mrs. Rose Heffron
J. Heupel
Mrs. Russell Henderly
Garry Herrmann
William Herbert
Mrs. Catherine Heyn
Mrs. Catherine Heyn, Sr.
Victor Henke
Joseph Heuermann
William Henges
Mrs. L. E. Hess

THE OLD: SYCAMORE STREET BASIN, WHERE NAVIGABLE CANAL ENDED AND BOATS TURNED AROUND.

THE NEW: CENTRAL PARKWAY, LOOKING FROM MAIN TO SYCAMORE STREET—BANFORD PHOTO.

Boys Dove for Coins When Beer Collector's Buggy Upset, Scattering $300 Into Canal!

"Hurrah! The beer collector's wagon has upset, dumping $300 in coins in the canal!

"Come on, boys! Let's dive for the money!"

This was the joyous shout that spread the tidings through the canal swimmers of fifty years ago that the muddy canal bottom was at last a silver mine. "Coin Divers' Night" happened only once in the history of the canal—so far as we know—but it was one of the grandest of nights for our divers!

John Wartmann, 706 Center street, Bellevue, Ky., relates the story: "In the late '70s or early '80s a beer collector of the Lion Brewery was returning to his brewery with his horse and buggy. On Logan street the horse was frightened and ran away, running over Logan and then over Liberty street. At the Liberty street bridge the buggy crashed and upset and a large quantity of money, with dollars and lots of small change like ten, twenty-five and fifty-cent pieces was scattered into the canal.

"A crowd gathered and you ought to have seen the boys diving for that money after school. When a diver came up he would hold up his hands and you could see some silver coins among a lot of mud! I tell you when it got toward evening that part of the canal was thick with people and boys diving for the coins—for in those days a nickel was a fortune for a lad."

Another canal swimmer, who was at the scene, writes: "When the Windisch-Muhlhauser buggy rolled into the canal about $300 in silver was scattered into the water. Everybody scrambled and dove into the water to get some of the coins. I recovered several dollars but they were taken away from me!"

Mrs. Phil Hirlinger
H. F. Hilge
C. A. Hilge
Anna Hirsch
Benjamin Hirsch
W. N. Hirst
Anthony Hinsen
Robert Hille
Miss Minnie Hornberger
Jacob Hoffmann
Louis Hornberger
H. C. Hoppe
Mrs. A. J. Hoyer
Henry Hohman
A. Frank Hoffmann
Fred Horstman
L. J. Hoff
Elizabeth Hottendorf
Dr. L. P. Hottendorf
W. N. Holmes
Clara Holmes
Joseph W. Hoffman
Roberta C. Hopkins
George J. Hoffman
George Hoff
Clifford D. Hoffner
Elmer F. Hunsicker
C. F. Huss
Otto Huber
William F. Huber
C. Hugo
Miss M. Huber
E. H. Hummel
J. M. Hughes, Jr.
Harry A. Huber
Fred W. Husman
Joe Illig
W. H. Ingram
Monroe Izor
George Jivoin
Matthew Jordan
C. J. John
Edward Jacob, Sr.
Matthew Jordan
Edward C. Jones
B. W. Johnson
Edward Jacob, Sr.
William E. James
George Jane
Mrs. George Jane
Clifford Jacobs

Howard H. Jacobs
Sam Jenike
Alvin H. Johnston
J. T. Johnson
R. W. Johnson
W. B. Jones
J. F. Jones
R. P. Jones
H. W. Joseph
Stella Johnston
Frank Jones, Sr.
Horace Johnson
Anthony Juengling
Nathan Jung
Dr. G. S. Junkerman
Charles A. Knorr
Al Keitel
B. H. Keller
Mrs. Marie Keller
Joseph Kouba
Frank Koebbing
Charles B. Ketterer
Charles H. Keith, Sr.
Mrs. Olive Koehler
Max Kuppner
George F. Kreh
Genevieve L. King
Gus C. Klinger
Harry Knodel
Mrs. Joseph F. Kouba
Nicholas Klein
Herman A. Krause
Val Kaiser
Henry A. Kasting
George Kaurish
E. B. Karrick
William Kamleiter
Mrs. Louise Kaiser
Emil Kaiser
Mrs. Chas. Keefe
Alonzo Kelly
Thomas Kehoe
Harold Keller
Charles Kern
Milton K. Kerlin
Rev. A. P. Keil
Dr. Walter Kent
Edwin Kiefer
Ralph Kittel
Walter Kittel
G. F. Kinzel
George Kinn

Harry Klein
Joseph Kleiner
Mrs. George Knapp
E. Koch
John Koch
Henry W. Kolling
Harold Korkes
John (Manny) Koch
John Knorr
John W. Knosp
Herman Knuepfer
W. C. Knodel
Felix Koch
Mrs. Belle T. Korte
Charles Kobmann
Arthur Kolbe
Mrs. Wm. Kollmann
Charles J. Krug
J. F. Krausser
Chris Krug
Frank Krippe
Mrs. Carrie Kramer
H. W. Krause
Joseph J. Kuntzler
J. J. Kushman
Frank Kuhn
Frank Kyrlach
Max C. Layritz
George J. Lecquire
Mrs. Julia E. Lamke
Sol J. Levi
William Leinen
Mrs. Wm. H. Lonney
Speaker Nicholas Longworth
Richard Ludeke
Charles G. Loge
A. F. Luebbing
Silas S. Lupton
John G. Linser, Sr.
Mrs. E. Lohr
Fred, William and Ed Ludwig
John G. Linser
Ferd L. Ludwig
George W. Lichtenfels
James E. Lightfield
Michael Laping
Stanley T. Lasonczyk
Silas S. Lapton
Joe Langelier
L. E. Langelier

George Lane
Thomas Langlier
Albert Lagaly
Mrs. Ella Lanter
Herman Lammars
Mrs. Margaretha Lanz
Chas. J. Lagemann
Warren E. Leavitt
John Lenert
Harry Letch
B. A Leonard
W. R. Lewis
H. LePris
A. F. Leue
George Lerch
Albert M. Linz
Charles Linser
Mrs. Wm. Linderman
J. G., A. E., and W. G. Lippelman
George Lippold
Chester A. Lishawa
William Licht
Adam Lotz
Herman Lowenstein
Henry Lohmann
Oscar Lotz
Mrs. Thomas Lynch
J. R. Lyon
Albert Lutz
Sam Ludwig, Sr.
August Bode Luckey
A. W. Macbrair
Herman J. Moeller
Mrs. Mears
Mrs. W. P. McCrone
Ed McCullough
James P. Morris
Joseph McClellan
Wm. A. Mundhenk
James P. Morris
James Meyers
Edw. J. Murphy, Sr.
Henry Mielke
H. E. Metz
Mrs. Bettie Mitchell
J. E. Meyers
Geo. H. Meinshausen
George A. Miller
James Meyer
A. J. (Tony) Mueller
N. E. Mathias

WHERE THOUSANDS ONCE SWAM! PARKWAY, LOOKING EAST FROM PLUM STREET—COMPARE WITH PHOTO ON PAGE 91.

Beautiful New Boulevard Cost $4,500,000

"The boulevard, Broadway to Ludlow avenue, is four and a half miles long and cost $4,500,000—a million a mile," said Chief Engineer Frank L. Raschig, of the Rapid Transit Commission, that built both boulevard and subway. "That figure includes the cost of property purchased.

"The rapid transit line, part subway and part in the open, is eleven miles long, the route leading through the city to St. Bernard and Norwood to Oakley. It is not altogether completed. The cost has been $6,500,000. This makes a total of $11,000,000. E. W. Edwards served as chairman of the commission from its beginning in 1915 to its end in 1928. The canal was drained here and 'went dry' October 22, 1919."

Opal Mason
F. C. Maisch
W. G. Maegly
Mathilda Maus
Charles R. Mauthe
Fred Martin
Mrs. E. B. Marlett
John E. Manthey
Phil Matre
Tom Martin
C. J. May
Matthew McBreen
Joe McCann
A. H. McClelland
Herman McFarland
Anson McKinney
M. B. McIntyre
Roger Meagher
Daniel Mersfelder
Clarence Messner
Arthur Mengebauer
Elmer Messner
A. F. Merland
Frank J. Meder
John Meyer
W. H. Miller
Frank Middeke
W. A. Minten
C. S. Mirick
Wm. Mischel
Mrs. Bettie Mitchell
W. T. Mitchell
C. S. Mirick
S. J. Mohr
C. D. Moore
A. F. Morrison
H. S. Mulford
Cris Mottern
G. J. Momberg
William Moschel
Roger Morrison
Mrs. Albert Mueller
William G. Munz
August L. Mueller
Ren Mulford, Jr.
Mr. and Mrs. Niemiller
Paul Naish
Arthur Neugebauer
Theo. S. Neekamp
Peter Niland
F. W. Niebling
Mrs. J. Naylor
Mrs. Lenora P. Neinberg
Herman Neal
W. J. Newton
Henry Newton
E. W. Nieder
Miss A. Nierman
Miss J. Nierman
W. J. Niederhelman
Edward Nowak
C. P. Noland
Dave Northman
George S. Noelfel
Mrs. Anna Noerman
Alban J. Norris
George Ochs
Gregg O'Leary
O. E. O'Neal
Fred F. Osterholz
I. A. Orth

Thomas B. Punshon
Charles Peterson, Sr.
Ed F. Petering
William Pattman
Louisa Munz Philipps
Henry Le Poris
Maj. J. J. Pontius
Henry Pell
John A. Prell
John W. Pons
William Patterson
Victor H. Pandorf
T. G. Paddack
Mrs. Richard Painer
Sam Pels
L. E. Peterson
Henry A. Peck
A. E. Peters
Charles Peterson
William Pfeiffer
G. C. Pfeiffer
Mrs. L. G. Piott
Dr. Carl A. Pleuger
Harry Plogman
Louis Plogsted
Warren W. Porter
Wm. Pohlking
Harry J. Punch
Mrs. Catherine L. Quaing
Edna B. Quick
Earl Quigley
William Rentrop
Charles Rentrop, Sr.
Milton Rosenberg
John Roehrer
Theodore Rolfes
Morris Rosenthal
C. T. Russell
John Roth
Helen Repasy
Walter Reemelin
C. A. Roos
William J. Trunnel
Arthur and Chester Ruhstaller
T. F. O'Reilly
L. W. Radina
"Rags, of Linn St."
Frank A. Raschig
Frank Ratterman
August J. Rames
J. H. Reis
Arnold Reif
Miss Lulu Reemelin
Lou F. Reemelin
William Rehse
William Reichman
Monk Reichel
George E. Renner
James S. Reynolds
George L. Reichl
Frank Rhein
Santford Richey
Conrad Richter
William Riemeier
Albert Ross
Israel Rosenstein
Mrs. Wm. Rosenzweig
J. H. Roncker
Albert Ross
Mrs. Adelaide Roth
Thomas Rogers

Frank S. Rohan
Thomas F. Rodgers
Harry Rentrop
Henry Ruhstaller
Fred Runk
Minnie Russe
John Ruckriegel
F. W. Ruthen
John F. Runnebaum
Henry Runnebaum
Harry Stangle
Harry R. Stevens
Sidney Spence
Louis Scheidt
George Schraffenberger, Jr.
G. A. Spoehrer
Mrs. J. Smith
W. A. Seibert
Arthur Schraffenberger
Joseph Schaiper
August W. Schuck
Joseph Sagmeister
Tirza Schraffenberger
Louis Scheidt
Fred A. Schroeder
Gustav L. Stecher
Philip Steffin
John B. Sander
H. P. Smith
Lee Stander
Edw. M. Scheid
Elmer Schulte
J. J. Schmidt
Anna M. Schlierf
August W. Schuck
Clarke C. Stayman
William H. H. Siles
Selma Salzman
Dr. William Sauter
William Sanders
Fred Sandman
L. A. Sauer
Arthur H. Sauer
Arthur H. Sander
Henry Schram
W. H. Schrader
A. Theo. Schulte
Jacob Schlachter
Walter R. Schellenberg
H. G. Schmidt
Hatty Scholl
Harry Schopper
A. B. Scherer
C. T. Schneider
Mrs. E. Schoenebaum
Louis Schoettinger
C. G. Scherer
Mrs. M. C. Scherer
Chas. Schweitzer
Jacob Schardt
Charles J. Schroeder
William A. Schwartz
John E. Scherer
Charles Schneider
Mrs. L. Schrantz
Mrs. Clara Schaum Sefton
Herman Seibert, Sr.
C. H. Sebastian
George Seibert

Paul Seward
Herman Seibert
W. J. Seller
George Sedgwick
Raymond Showell
Christian Shook
H. W. Shoup
Lee Shohl
C. F. Shield
Dr. L. K. Shepherd
Oscar L. Shafer
Frank Silz
H. C. Sims
Sam Singer
Dr. W. H. Siehl
Anna Bell Siles
Fred J. Silberhorn
C. W. Skillman
Jim Slattery
Ed. V. Smith
Mrs. Joanna E. Smith
C. A. Smithner
Mrs. J. Smith
William Smiley
Dr. E. B. Snyder
A. R. Snyder
M. B. Sohmer
C. L. Soetje
A. Spitzmiller
F. B. Spangler
W. P. Spangler
Charles Spring
Charles P. Stamm
W. B. Stewart
H. R. Stewart
A. C. Stewart
F. W. Strubbe
Mrs. Francis L. Steffens
Harry R. Stevens
Philip Steffin
F. W. Strubbe
John P. Steinmuller
Henry Schram
Jacob Staigle
Lee Stander
J. L. Stix
Edward Strumpler
O. F. Stothfang
T. E. Sturr
Peter B. Steil
R. G. Steidinger
Jacob Staigler
L. Straley
William A. Stein
E. W. Stemler
Wm. Strohfeldt
Walter E. Streng
J. C. Schwenkmeyer
C. G. Stewart
Horace K. Stueve
Phillip Steinmetz
Roy Stephens
O. A. Stemler
Joe Steele
Mrs. Nancy Switzer
Mrs. William Switzer
Paul Sweeney
Neil C. Sullivan
Chas. Tatgenhorst, Jr.
Frank C. Turner
Chief Justice William H. Taft

SWIMMING HOLE GONE! PARKWAY, LOOKING NORTH FROM PLUM ST. BEND.—BANFORD PHOTO.

Boulder Tied in Bather's Clothing, Then—Kerplunk!

A boy bet he could swim from Wade street to Findlay. In his absence another youngster wrapped a boulder in his shirt and another in his trousers and threw both into the canal. On his return the swimmer looked for his clothing and could not find it. The perpetrator of the outrage was particularly zealous and sympathetic in assisting him. Jimmy, after a fruitless search, concluded he had better go home. About 9 p. m., Jimmy went down Wade street on the run, the gang in hot pursuit.

Unencumbered, Jimmy made fast time and left the gang behind. German citizens, sitting on the doorsteps, were astonished when a Godiva-like phantom whizzed past, to be followed by a crowd of lusty-lunged youngsters.

Jimmy reached home and explained. The gang arrived and commenced, "Chaw, chaw, green apples." A window went up and a bucket of water came down. The gang dispersed.—H. Schroer, M.D., John street and Bauer avenue.

Found Bag of Counterfeit Silver Dollars in Canal

"One day I found a salt bag full of counterfeit silver dollars under the Main street bridge," writes a friend. "It was evidently thrown into the canal by a bunch of counterfeiters. I thought I had a treasure—but a man from the Courthouse took the dollars from me and chopped them up with a hatchet!"

One day the canal was so thickly filled with fish that we picked them up by the bucket fulls.—John E. Manthey.

Lockland Canal Collector

C. W. Skillman—I was canal tolls collector at Lockland for eighteen years and now, at 78, my mind is filled with happy memories of the canal in its busy early days. As a youth I drove the mules and was boat steersman. At 16 I had a memorable ride on a canal boat to Cincinnati—to buy an alto horn! And I played gloriously on it in the band, for years! Ah, the sweet recollections of that canal!

Herbert R. Hopkins writes from St. Louis telling how a policeman captured the clothing of a group of swimmers at the Twelfth street bridge, made the boys dress and took them to the station—all except one boy, who ran eight blocks to his home, unobserved by the policeman. So the officer had one extra suit of clothes left over. He thought the missing boy was drowned and made out a report on the "drowning." Next morning the boy's mother called for his clothes—and the "drowning" was erased from the records.

I fell into the canal three times as a child, and was thrice rescued. Perhaps this is a record for a woman member of the Canal Club. I spent my happy childhood along the canal.—Mrs. J. Smith, St. Bernard.

I was caught on the old Mohawk Bridge when it arose to let the boats pass under and failed to come down.—Miss Helen Repasy.

My last experience on the canal was forty-five years ago when I skated out to Wyoming on a bitter cold Sunday to see a young lady who is my wife today.—Charles H. Sebastian.

John Theobald
James Terwillegar
F. Tedesche
Edwin C. Trauth
Mrs. George Tolken
William Teichman
Alma Pons Taylor
D. E. Taylor
Mrs. J. N. Taylor
Mrs. A. Taylor
J. W. Taggart
Arthur A. Taylor
Richard I. Thole
Hugh R. Thompson
Joseph G. Thill
George H. Tow
Edythe Tolken
George Tolken
Mrs. Viola Tobertga
Edwin Tompkins
Mary Toedt
Christa Toedt
William Toedt
Charles Toedt
Morris Tobias
Robert Toepfert

W. D. Troy
Frank Tullis
Mrs. Belle Dickman Tullis
Howard Turrel
W. C. Tyirin
Thos. Underwood
Dr. H .O. Valentiner
A. C. Volkman
Mrs. Martha Vogel
R. D. Van Fossen
Charles Vaughan
Walter G. Volz
Raymond B. Volker
Gussie N. Voss
Alice M. Voorhees
Mrs. Susan Vogel
Charles Weik and and Brothers
William Werner
George Woesner
Walter C. Wurster
Emerson Walker
W. H. F. Whiteford
J. O. Wright
Andy Wachter

Alfred S. Wood
Mrs. Lenora Painer Weinberg
W. M. Wagner
Ed Walsh
John Wartmann
William R. Walsh
Emerson Walker
Charles Walther
A. C. Wagner
John Warthman
H. R. Wellman
A. J. Weichold
Gustav R. Werner
L. J. Weiss
C. J. Wenderoth
Don C. Welch
J. B. Wetterer
John Wetterer
Samuel Wertheimer
Clifford F. Weber
Emil Wendel
Arthur Wern
G. L. Wergers
Henry W. Wendt
Theo Werner, Jr.

Clifford F. Weber
G. W. Winall
C. F. Widman
J. Widmer
C. J. Winnes
Mrs C. J. Winnes
E. F. Wirthwine
Fred Willet
Thomas Winter
Fred Wiebking
J. W. Wilder
Frank R. Williams
Dr. B. A. Williams
Duke Williamson
Joseph A. Wittrock
Mrs. Amelia Wicker
Charles L. Wiebold
Al H. Wilhelm
Charles Wise
William C. Winans
Henry Wolf
W. C. Wurster
G. W. Yates
Margaret Yeager
Peter Young
Ralph J. Zevy
Edward J. Zeller

CANAL BOAT PRISCILLA ON LAST EXCURSION!

Here's the pretty excursion canal boat Priscilla on the last trip along the old towpath. The boat, drawn by three mules and a tractor, was one of the most attractive floats in the Central Parkway dedication parades. The crew consisted of Fred L. Schille, president of the Findlay Market Association, that built the float; Chester A. Lathrop, John Ehman and Clarence Stegner, with Charles Ludwig, Canal Scribe, as steersman. The charming passengers, clad in costumes of the olden days, were: Catherine Henz, Edna Aver, Ann Lindhorst, Audrey McKee and Elizabeth Katzler. The Schnapps Band, with Whitey Ahrens, Teddy Lieberth and Dave Davidorf, provided music continuously from Sycamore Basin to Second Basin!—Photo by Roy Tichenor.

Both Fell In!

We would hire a motor boat for a day, ride for miles, find a nice, cool spot and each lunch. It was great! I fell in with my best Sunday-school dress, and my husband fell through the ice! So we're both members.—Mrs. Margaret Bohnenkamp.

Vine Street Astronomer

Remember the old astronomer who stood on the Vine street bridge with his telescope and permitted people to view the moon through it for five cents?—Canal Swimmer.

At Grant street one day I was attracted by the cries of a man who had partaken too freely of the cup that cheers, and had decided to walk upon the waters of the canal for a short cut in the direction of his habitat. I appeared in time to pull him out.—A. F. Morrison.

Here's a record: I broke through eight-inch ice January 12, 1912, when it was eight above zero!—Frank R. Williams.

I swam in the canal over a thousand times.—Henry A. Peck.

SPRAY! ALL THAT'S LEFT OF THE DEAR OLD CANAL!

Where thousands once swam, Joe Banford, our photographer, and I found these boys on the Parkway sprinkling each other with the gardener's hose! We used to be chased for swimming in the canal without bathing suits. These lads had suits—but no canal to swim in! Times change—but boys' love of water play remains the same! . . .

And having come to this last page, I longed to see the waters of the old canal once more. Many readers, too, would no doubt like to know where to find the remnants of the stream. So, with Mrs. Ludwig, who assisted in the preparation of this book, I motored out to Lockland, March 3, 1929—and, lo!—there was much storm water in the canal and the old locks. And in the State House at the locks we found Horace Johnson, canal caretaker, and the veteran canal captain, Joe Butler, who nearly wept as he told us how his fleet of steel canal boats had been shipped away to Chicago. Three miles above Lockland we saw the canal in its pristine beauty, a lovely stream in the woodlands—and walked along the towpath till we came to a break in the canal bank, where the water escaped to Millcreek. A few miles on and we saw the canal again at Crescentville, and saw a huge dead carp in the water—mill there—and saw the last surviving canal boat in Hamilton County, Capt. Butler's West Carrollton, a steel hull rusting in the water. And a few miles north of Glendale, on the Princeton road, we saw the canal again at Port Union and there met Judge Ellis B. Gregg, owner of the beautiful Ellis Lake, twenty miles from Cincinnati—the closest remaining canal lake. Mud bars prevented a full flow of water coming down the canal from the Big Miami River—but the water was sparklingly clear! We could see the stones at the bottom, and the boys said they fished, swam, boated and skated along the canal!

The rippling waters, the graceful sweep of the canal through pleasant countryside, the pretty, tree-lined towpath, no longer trodden by mules and with a forest growing on its edges, brought a flood of happy memories! Yes, all things have their day and pass away!

Farewell, Towpath, Friend to us all,
In summer, winter, spring and fall,
Our Happy Playground all year through!
And goodby, Playmates! Luck to you!

www.ingramcontent.com/pod-product-compliance
Lightning Source LLC
Chambersburg PA
CBHW080025130526
44591CB00037B/2671

www.ingramcontent.com/pod-product-compliance
Lightning Source LLC
Chambersburg PA
CBHW080025130526
44591CB00037B/2671